Contents

Acknowledgements

The *Quality in Diversity* framework has been produced by the collaboration of a very considerable number of early childhood professionals, including the project team based at Goldsmiths' College, University of London, the project steering group, the three writing groups, the editorial group and representatives of the member organisations of the Early Childhood Education Forum. Their names are listed below.

Project Team 1993-7
Vicky Hurst, Director (Coordinator 0-3), Goldsmiths' College
Marjorie Ouvry, Project Associate (Coordinator 3-5), Goldsmiths' College
Celia Burgess-Macey, Project Associate (Coordinator 5-8), Goldsmiths' College

Steering Group
Pat Davies, Children in Wales
Pat Dench, PLA
Susan Hay, CCA
Ann Jamieson, National Children's Bureau (chair 1997-8)
Jenefer Joseph/Florence Beetlestone, TACTYC
Annabel Lewis, OMEP
Serena Johnson, High/Scope
Christine Pascal, Worcester College of Education
Gillian Pugh, National Children's Bureau (chair 1993-7)
Greta Sandler/Jane Lane, EYTARN
Wendy Scott, BAECE/Early Education (acting chair 1997)
Dorothy Selleck, National Children's Bureau

Project Editor
Mary Jane Drummond, School of Education, University of Cambridge

Working Group 0-3
Sue Banfield, Association of Metropolitan Authorities (AMA)*
Meg Bender, PLA
Helen Carless, Headteacher, co-opted
Pat Cave, BAECE
Lucy Davies, EYTARN
Sally Davies, South Glamorgan Social Services
Bernadette Duffy, NANC*
Peter Elfer, National Children's Bureau*
Maureen Gard and Ann Burton, NPDNA
Sue Griffin, NCMA*

Susan Hay, Childcare and Education Association*
Lauren Joffe, Montessori Education UK*
Wendy Jory, Senior Inspector and Sue Banfield, AMA
Margaret Kinsey, Gwent LEA
Joyce Kuzbyt, BAECE
Ann Leonard, co-opted
Kalvinder Lewis, co-opted*
Lin Marsh, AAUEF
Janet Morris, OMEP*
Margaret Parker, AMA
Greta Sandler, EYTARN*
Mollie White, NPA*
Tracey Wilkes-Green, Associate for Susan Hay
Patricia Winifred, co-opted

Working Group 3-5
Davina Adebowale, co-opted
Ann Beadle, NPDNA
Paddy Beales, BAECE
Maxine Bretherton Budd/Jeanne Morrison, AMA
Ann Davies, AMA
Alex Duncan, Association of County Councils (ACC)
Janet Dye, NEYN
Ann Greenwood, AMA
Ann Henderson, PLA*
Sharon Hogan, AMA*
Anne Jalim, ACC
Jenefer Joseph, TACTYC
Pam Lafferty, High/Scope
Branwen Llewellyn Howells, Headteacher, Merthyr Tydfil
Anne McMullan and Joy Roberts, AMA
Rita Miller and Maureen Sinnot, AMA
Jeanne Morrison, AMA
Viv Murphy, NANC
Nenetia Nelson, co-opted
Hilary Pauley, CCA
Barbara Powell, AMA
Dorothy Selleck, National Children's Bureau*
Victoria Sheridan, Montessori Education UK*
Kath Shorten, NAEIAC*
Peggy Sleight, AMA*
Laura Timms, OMEP*
Judy Warner, NCMA*
Irene Westerman, NPA/Mencap

Working Group 5-8
Geva Blenkin, TACTYC
Carole Burton-Collis, NCMA
Lisa Capper, Kids' Clubs Network*
Diane Dolley, Sandwell Metropolitan LEA*
Mary Jane Drummond, School of Education, University of Cambridge*
Mark Evans, ACC
Yvette Evans, EYTARN
Julie Fisher, BAECE
Margaret Heard, Warwickshire County Education Authority*
Ron Hiley, CCA
Pauline Hoey, NAEIAC
Rhianwen Huws Roberts, Curmni Cynnal, C Gwynedd and Isle of Anglesey
Annabel Lewis, OMEP
Daryll Luxford, NPDNA
Jackie Naraynsingh, Manchester Children's Services*
Ann Nelson, Coventry LEA*
Usha Sahni, co-opted
Maggie Walker, Kids' Clubs Network
Helen Wheatley, Montessori Education UK*
Marian Whitehead, EYCG
* = members of writing groups

In addition, grateful thanks are due to many individuals in the early childhood community who have generously given their time and their critical support.

Rashida Baig	Gulzar Kanji
Margaret Carr	John Matthews
Jacqui Cousins	Christine Morgan
Dawn Davis	Gerry Mulhearn
Margaret Fairclough	Rosemary Murphy
Mary Head	Angela Peart
Elaine Herbert	Bobbie Stanley
Sally Jenkinson	Marcia Thompson
Carolyn Jones	Olivia Vincenti
Jane Lane	

We are grateful to the Department for Education and Employment for their financial support in the final stages of the project.

The *Quality in Diversity* framework went through many drafts before publication, and the technical support it has received throughout its history has been of the highest quality. We are greatly indebted to:

Dee Seymour and Joan Callan at Goldsmiths' College
Ann Robinson, Annie Sampford and Gillian Potkins at the Early Childhood Unit, National Children's Bureau

Finally, sincere thanks to the Bernard van Leer Foundation for their belief in the value of this project, and the funding that made it possible.

Preface
The Early Childhood Education Forum

The Early Childhood Education Forum is a consortium of the major national organisations concerned with the care and education of young children. It was established in January 1993. Member organisations represent statutory provision in education and social services, the voluntary and private sectors, services for children with special educational needs, parents, governors, advisors, inspectors and local authorities. A list of the current members, almost all of whom have contributed to this framework, is given overleaf.

A first priority of the Forum was to agree a set of aims - not as easy as it might appear, as is evident from the sentence in our original document which reads:

> Although individual member organisations of the Forum represent a range of different interests and will wish to emphasise different aspects of early years work, our over-riding concern is to work together and speak with a united voice in pursuit of our overall goals.

It was possible, after some discussion about the word 'quality', to agree on the following:

> The Forum believes that all children have a right to good quality care and education in their early years, and points to research that shows that investment in services at this stage has beneficial long-term educational, social and economic results.

We aim:
- to raise public awareness of the needs of young children;

- to seek a more appropriate share of resources for early years services, and the transfer of some existing resources to the early years;

- to work towards developing common standards, based on developmentally appropriate care and education, across all services for young children;

- to seek access to appropriate training for all early years educators;

- to speak with one voice for children.

The underpinning principles upon which the Forum is founded are derived from *Investing in Young Children: Costing an education and day care service*, Holtermann (1992) published by the National Children's Bureau in association with the local authority associations and the voluntary sector.

They are that:

- Young children are important in their own right and as a resource for the future.

- Young children are to be valued; their full development is possible only if they live in an environment that reflects and respects their individual identity, culture and heritage.

- Parents are primarily responsible for nurturing and supporting the development of their children and this important role should be more highly valued by society.

- Central and local government have a duty, working in partnership with parents, to ensure that services and support are available for families - services that encourage children's cognitive, social, emotional and physical development and meet parents' need for support for themselves and day care for their children.

The Forum also endorses the principles of children's upbringing and education stated in the UN Convention on the Rights of the Child, and ratified by UK government (United Nations 1989). Article 29 of the Convention states that:

1. Parties agree that the education of the child shall be directed to:

    (a) the development of the child's personality, talents and mental and physical abilities to their fullest potential;

    (b) the development of respect for human rights and fundamental freedoms, and for the principles enshrined in the Charter of the United Nations;

    (c) the development of respect for the child's parents, his or her own cultural identity, language and values, for the national values of the country in which the child is living, the country from which he or she may originate and for civilizations different from his or her own;

    (d) the preparation of the child for responsible life in a free society, in the spirit of understanding, peace, tolerance, equality of sexes, and friendship among all peoples, ethnic, national and religious groups and persons of indigenous origin;

    (e) the development of respect for the natural environment.

In the first three years of its existence the Forum has worked on many national issues, through the whole Forum and through sub-groups on policy, curriculum, inspection and training. This framework is the outcome of its most ambitious project, but it has also recently published *Education and Training for Work in the Early Years* (Pugh 1996). The Forum continues to discuss issues of national importance for early childhood care and education with ministers and opposition spokespersons, with officials from the Department of Education and Employment, and Department of Health, with SCAA and OFSTED (who have observers on the Forum) and with other national bodies whose work impinges on the lives of young children and those who work with them.

Gillian Pugh

Chair, Early Childhood Education Forum 1993 - 1997

Member organisations of the Early Childhood Education Forum who endorse *Quality in Diversity*

Association of Advisers for Under Eights and Their Families (AAUEF)
Association of Educational Psychologists (AEP)
British Association for Early Childhood Education (BAECE/Early Education)
Campaign for State Education (CASE)
Childcare and Education Association (CCA) (until 1997)
Children in Scotland
Children in Wales
Commission for Racial Equality (CRE)
Council for Awards in Children's Care and Education (CACHE)
Council for Disabled Children (CDC)
Daycare Trust (DCT)
Early Years Curriculum Group (EYCG)
Early Years Trainers Anti-Racist Network (EYTARN)
High/Scope UK
Incorporated Association of Preparatory Schools (IAPS)
Local Government Association (LGA)
Mencap
Montessori Education UK
National Association of Education Inspectors, Advisors and Consultants (NAEIAC)
National Association of Headteachers (NAHT)
National Association of Nurseries in Colleges, Universities (NANCU)
National Association of Nursery Centres (NANC)
National Childminding Association (NCMA)
National Children's Bureau (NCB)
National Council of Parent Teacher Associations (NCPTA)
National Early Years Network (NEYN)
National Portage Association (NPA)
National Private Day Nurseries Association (NPDNA)
National Union of Teachers (NUT)
Pre-school Learning Alliance (PLA)
Save the Children (SCF)
The Early Years Organisation (NIPPA)
Tutors of Advanced Courses for Teachers of Young Children
 (The Professional Association of Early Childhood Educators) (TACTYC)
World Organisation for Early Childhood Education
 (Organisation Mondiale pour l'Education Préscolaire - OMEP)
Working for Childcare (WFC)

Section One
Introducing *Quality in Diversity*

What is *Quality in Diversity*?

Quality in Diversity is a framework to enable early childhood practitioners to think about, understand, support and extend the learning of young children from birth to the age of eight. It builds on the existing expertise and experience of people working in a wide range of settings, in order to create a shared language for all early years practitioners, to help them deepen their understanding of how young children learn, and to unify and consolidate the strengths of diverse settings and approaches. The framework represents a new coherence in the thinking of early years practitioners. It is the outcome of an unprecedented coming together of different organisations and different traditions, who have found, within the themes of quality and diversity, a new way of speaking with one voice in the interests of all young children.

Why have we written *Quality in Diversity*?

The last 20 years have seen many changes in the lives of young children, their families and the services that many of them attend.

- Family patterns are changing. Parents are having fewer children. An increasing rate of divorce and remarriage means that many children are growing up with a lone parent or step-parent, and with siblings who may be step-brothers and sisters.

- Roles within families and the circumstances of families' lives are changing in response to employment and unemployment patterns, with more women returning to the workforce or to study, and many families experiencing the hardship of unemployment and poverty.

- Britain is becoming an increasingly varied and diverse society, with a richness in cultures, languages, religions, and ethnicities and in approaches to bringing up children. Policies, procedures and practices have had to be developed to take account of this diversity. Britain is also an unequal society in which many children experience discrimination and prejudice. It is therefore necessary to take positive action to promote a respect for this diversity and to counter discrimination and the learning of negative attitudes to differences in people.

- Increasing numbers of young children are experiencing day care and early education in a very wide range of settings (of variable quality) outside the home before they start formal schooling.

- A number of significant pieces of legislation have impacted on the way in which early childhood practitioners support young children's care and learning in these settings:
  • the Education Reform Act 1988 which introduced the National Curriculum for children of five and upwards, and a new system of school inspection through OFSTED;

  • the 1989 Children Act, which provided a new regulatory framework and inspection framework for social services, private and voluntary sector care for children under eight;

  • the 1996 Nursery Education and Grant-Maintained Schools Act introduced Ofsted inspections for nursery schools and enabled the government to put in place new systems for funding an expansion of early years education (initially for four-year-olds). These developments were linked to *Desirable Outcomes for Children's Learning on Entering Compulsory Education* (SCAA 1996), a document to be used both as the basis for inspection of the full range of settings available to four-year-olds, and by the practitioners in those settings.

- Other recent legislation provides for the identification of unlawful discrimination in both the employment of staff and in the way early years services are delivered:
  • the 1970 Equal Pay Act, the 1975 and 1986 Sex Discrimination Acts, the 1976 Race Relations Act and the 1995 Disability Discrimination Act.

- The development of a system of National Vocational Qualifications in child care and education has created a means of awarding qualifications on the basis of assessment of competence, through a mix of formal training, informal learning, experience and development of personal maturity. This system has still to be completed and funding for the necessary training and assessment remains patchy.

- Discussions are ongoing about the future of teacher education, including the initial and in-service training of those who will teach children in infant and nursery classes

- From September 1998, there will be a new requirement for Baseline Assessment to be carried out with children in their first term at school.

Against this wide ranging backdrop of change, and in spite of a welcome recognition of the importance of early care and education, many early childhood practitioners have felt that the needs of young children and their families have been overlooked. There has been serious concern that developments within the wider education system - in relation to curriculum, assessment, inspection and the education of teachers - have not been built either on an understanding of how young children learn or on existing best practice in early childhood settings. It was this concern, together with the bringing together of representatives of all those who work with young children within the Early Childhood Education Forum, that led to the setting up of the *Quality in Diversity* project.

Who has written *Quality in Diversity*?

The development of *Quality in Diversity* has been a genuinely collaborative enterprise, involving the member organisations of the Early Childhood Education Forum listed in the Preface. With the support of a generous grant from the Bernard van Leer Foundation, a team based at Goldsmiths' College has undertaken the bulk of the work, coordinating the efforts of 80 nominated representatives of the ECEF member organisations, and supported by a steering group drawn from the membership of the Forum. The final editing of the framework has been undertaken at the Early Childhood Unit of the National Children's Bureau.

How did we write *Quality in Diversity*?

The project started from the underpinning principles of the Early Childhood Education Forum.

The Forum endorses the following principles with regard to children's learning:

- Learning begins at birth.

- Care and education are inseparable - quality care is educational and quality education is caring.

- Every child develops at his or her own pace, but adults can stimulate and encourage learning.

- All children benefit from developmentally appropriate care and education.

- Skilled and careful observation is the key to helping children learn.

- Cultural and physical diversity should be respected and valued: a proactive anti-bias approach should be adopted and stereotypes challenged.

- Learning is holistic and cannot be compartmentalised: trust, motivation, interest, enjoyment and physical and social skills are as important as purely cognitive gains.

- Young children learn best through play, first hand experience and talk.

- Carers and educators should work in partnership with parents, who are their children's first educators.

- Quality care and education require well-trained educators/carers and on-going training and support.

In drawing on the experience of the member organisations, it was also important to build on the many documents already produced by practitioners through their national organisations - for example, guidance from many local education authorities, the publications of the Pre-school Learning Alliance, National Childminding Association and Kids' Clubs Network. The National Curriculum programmes of study and the *Desirable Outcomes* documents (SCAA 1996/CAAW 1996) were also used, to ensure continuity in thinking about provision for children from birth to eight, through the period when children enter school, until the beginning of Key Stage Two. At an early stage, therefore, the project team set about collecting, collating and analysing examples of existing 'best practice'. A list of the local authorities and organisations who contributed publications at this stage is given in Appendix 2

At the same time, three groups were set up drawn from the nominated representatives of the member organisations of ECEF. One group developed the framework as it related to children under three, one for children three to five, and one for children from five to eight. These broadly based groups, and in particular the small sub-groups that took responsibility for the writing, formed the backbone of the project. They met separately and together during the course of the project, working and reworking the central concepts of the project, and bringing examples of practice from their diverse settings to contribute to the final document.

In the final stage of the project, a completed draft of the framework was sent to 300 practitioners, advisers, officers, consultants, academics and researchers, reflecting the diversity of early childhood settings in England and Wales. These people were invited to read and to work with the completed document during the spring of 1997; extensive, encouraging and critical feedback was received from groups and individuals, and has been of great importance in producing this, the published version.

Why is it called *Quality in Diversity*?

The title of the framework introduces the two guiding themes of the project: the two words, *quality* and *diversity*, represent the most firmly held aspirations of all those involved in developing the framework.

Quality: the Early Childhood Education Forum, and all its member organisations, are committed to the importance of high quality educational provision in settings for young children. The principle of quality, rooted in a commitment to equality, is not negotiable. Young children's learning, from birth to eight, deserves the very best services, and the most highly skilled practitioners, that a society can provide. This shared commitment to quality runs through the framework as a whole. It has been developed to support practitioners in their central task: putting their commitment to quality into practice, ensuring quality in educational settings for children from birth to eight.

Diversity: the members of the Early Childhood Education Forum are equally committed to the concept of diversity. We know and understand the many characteristics of early learning that are common to all children; but we also recognise and value *individual differences* between children.

This aspect of diversity includes children's different abilities, dispositions, aptitudes and needs.

In this framework, other aspects of diversity are also important. The framework recognises the importance for early years practitioners of recognising the *diversity of children's families and communities*, their social, ethnic/racial, cultural, religious and linguistic groups and identities.

Furthermore, the framework is based on an assumption of *diversity in the settings* in which children are cared for and educated. Here the term diversity refers to the different educational approaches and philosophies that underpin early childhood practice. The adults who work in early years settings have different qualifications and training experiences, different traditions and different priorities, and so meet the needs of the families they serve in a variety of ways. The Early Childhood Education Forum was itself founded in acknowledgement of this diversity. But diversity need not mean antagonism; in this framework, agreement on quality and recognition of diversity go hand in hand. The framework represents the quintessence of what early childhood practitioners can all agree on, and endorses the ways in which we can agree to differ.

What is *Quality in Diversity* for?

The framework as a whole is a working document that will help early childhood practitioners to apply their present knowledge and understanding, so that their expertise is put to good use in the care and education of children under eight.

Because it has been developed by early years practitioners, the framework builds on existing expertise and experience. But it also has something new to offer. It offers us a way of seeing more fully, understanding more clearly, and valuing more explicitly the richness and complexity of children's learning. It offers a way of articulating more rigorously the tasks of early childhood practitioners, and their awesome responsibilities for young children and their learning.

The framework is, in a sense, a set of tools with different purposes:

- a torch, with which we can see more clearly what happens in early childhood settings;

- a map, with which we can explore different possibilities in our work with children;

- a balance, with which we can check the variety and quality of the experiences we offer children;

- a microscope, with which to examine the fine detail of children's learning and experiences;

- a spirit level, with which to check the solidity of the foundations being laid for children's later learning;

- a handle, with which we can grasp more firmly the concepts of quality and equality, bringing a stronger understanding of what these terms mean into children's lives.

But the framework is not a tool that can be used to turn out identical copies of an original form: it is not a photocopier or a pastry cutter. The *Quality in Diversity* project members did not work together to specify an early years curriculum for all; noone in the early years community wants the curriculum of every early years setting to be identical. Diversity is a necessary condition of quality in services for young children.

What does the *Quality in Diversity* framework consist of?

There are three main elements in the framework.

- The **FOUNDATIONS for early learning** - five key ideas that are integral to worthwhile learning in the early years.

- **GOALS for early learning** - more detailed descriptions of what the foundations mean in terms of children's learning. The foundations and goals are presented and illustrated in Section Two.

- **CHILDREN'S ENTITLEMENTS** - the conditions that will ensure that the foundations for early learning are firmly established for every child, in every different setting. These entitlements are described in Section Three.

- These three elements are used together, in Section Four, to examine the part that practitioners play in children's learning, from birth to eight. A description of the principal responsibilities of early years practitioners is given in the form of a simple diagram - the **PRACTITIONER'S WHEEL**.

- In Section Five, examples are given of ways in which practitioners used the framework, during the trialing period, to examine and develop their practice.

- The Appendices contain a full list of the organisations represented in the Early Childhood Education Forum, a list of the publications contributed by ECEF members at the start of the *Quality in Diversity* project and a list of suggested further reading.

Who is *Quality in Diversity* for?

Quality in Diversity has been written by early childhood practitioners for early childhood practitioners. It is intended for all those who work in

combined nursery centres
community nurseries
early years units
family centres
homes (childminders and nannies)

hospital schools
maintained nursery, infant, special, first and
primary schools
nursery centres and classes
opportunity groups

out of school clubs
play centres
playbuses
pre-schools and playgroups

private day nurseries
private schools
social service day nurseries
workplace creches

Although it is intended primarily for practitioners, at each point it builds on the role that parents and other carers are already playing, and will continue to play, as their children's continuing educators.

How can *Quality in Diversity* be used?

The framework is intended to support practitioners in their work and to stimulate their thinking. It can be used as a working document in a variety of ways, some of which are illustrated in detail in Section Five, and some more briefly in Sections Two, Three and Four.

Ways of using the framework by the staff of a single early years setting could include:

- using the **FOUNDATIONS for early learning** as a starting point for revisiting and re-examining existing curriculum documents or mission statements.

- using single elements of the **FOUNDATIONS** to check for quality across one week's work in the setting, or against a set of observations of one child's experiences.

- using the **FOUNDATIONS** to identify areas of practice that might need more careful scrutiny or fresh thinking.

- using the **GOALS for early learning** to monitor individual children, or groups of children, drawing on a collection of observations.

- using the **ENTITLEMENTS** to monitor aspects of adult provision and interaction that may be giving cause for concern.

- using **FOUNDATIONS, GOALS** and **ENTITLEMENTS** to put together a rounded account of how the setting as a whole meets its responsibilities for young children's care, learning and well-being - an account for a managing committee, for governors, for community groups.

All of these activities could involve parents and other family members.

Ways of using the framework by the staff of more than one setting, in one or more shared staff development sessions, could include the following.

- Using one or more of the **FOUNDATIONS** and **GOALS** to compare and contrast different approaches. Selected observations could be made to enable practitioners to identify and justify the *diversity* in their practice of *quality*.

- Using the **ENTITLEMENTS** to investigate issues of quality and equality, by collecting selected observations of children of different ages, in different settings.

- Using the **PRACTITIONER'S WHEEL** to explore differences and similarities in the practitioners' approaches to their central tasks.

- Using selected parts of the framework, by agreement, as the focus for an exchange of visits and observations across a variety of settings, and to stimulate professional study and research.

What is different about *Quality in Diversity*?

There are, of course, other approaches to early childhood education. In this country alone, thinking about the care and education of young children under eight is, in various settings, structured by, for example:

- the National Curriculum (DES/Welsh Office 1995);

- *Desirable Outcomes for Children's Learning* (SCAA 1996/CAAW 1996);

- *Looking at Children's Learning* (SCAA 1997);

- areas of learning and experience (DES/HMI 1989);

- areas of development: physical, intellectual, emotional, social, linguistic/ communicative (derived from the work of Susan Isaacs 1930, 1933).

There are also the publications of organisations such as the Pre-school Learning Alliance, the National Childminding Association, Kids' Clubs Network, Montessori Education UK, the Steiner Waldorf Fellowship, the Commission for Racial Equality, High/Scope and Mudiad Ysgolion Meithrin, together with an enormous number of curriculum documents developed by teams of practitioners and advisers in local authorities. There are also the requirements of the *Code of Practice on the Identification and Assessment of Special Educational Needs* (DfE 1994) and guidance which accompanies the Children Act (Department of Health 1991).

The *Quality in Diversity* framework has been developed to strengthen and enrich these current approaches. It is intended to be complementary to what already exists, and in no way a competing alternative.

Most importantly, the framework does not set out to specify a curriculum, or a pre-school curriculum, or even a pre-pre-school curriculum. It offers, instead, a way of thinking about learning that will help practitioners shape their own quality curriculum for the care and education of children from birth to eight.

Whereas the National Curriculum programmes of study, and the *Desirable Outcomes* document, describe children's achievements in terms of knowledge, concepts, skills and attitudes, this framework aspires to do something different but complementary. The **FOUNDATIONS** and **GOALS**, taken as a whole, describe the children themselves. They are a way of thinking about the most important characteristics of the lives of young learners.

When these learners are of statutory school age, they will be actively studying the nine subjects of the National Curriculum and religious education; when they are four- or five-years-old, they may be active in the six areas of learning described in *Desirable Outcomes*; but throughout this period, and before, from birth to eight, they will also be - as the **FOUNDATIONS** describe them - belonging, thinking, imagining, contributing, expressing, connecting, participating: living and learning. These aspects of learning underpin all later learning, which is why they have been referred to in this framework as **FOUNDATIONS**.

A note on the examples
The illustrative examples used in this document were contributed by members of the *Quality in Diversity* project. They were collected in a wide variety of settings from across the country, reflecting both the mixed membership of the project and the central themes of *quality* and *diversity*. In the text, the examples have been presented with the minimum of contextual background, and are not attributed to the precise locality, or the type of provision from which they came. This is to focus attention on the particular aspects of quality and diversity under discussion, and to demonstrate that quality in early years provision is nobody's monopoly.

In this relatively short document, it is not possible to include examples of children from all the various cultural groups living in Britain today. The examples selected are intended to reflect the spirit, if not the representative detail, of this welcome diversity.

Conclusion

This section has introduced the framework and its component parts, together with an account of the context in which it was written, and the purposes for which it is intended.

In summary *Quality in Diversity*:

- creates a shared language for all early years practitioners;

- unifies and consolidates the strengths of diverse settings and approaches;

- extends practitioners' understanding of children's learning;

- complements current approaches;

- deepens practitioners' understanding of their responsibilities for children's learning;

- traces the continuum of children's learning from birth to eight;

- values collaboration between practitioners as a means of enhancing quality;

- expresses its authors' commitment to the principles of *quality* and *diversity*.

Description of terms

Throughout *Quality in Diversity* we use a number of words that can have different interpretations. Our use of these words is as follows:

Challenging prejudice, bias, stereotyping and discrimination: the resources, policies, practices and procedures by which practitioners recognise and confront these major obstacles to equality. Prejudice, bias, stereotyping and discrimination may appear in many forms, on a variety of grounds (including aptitude, ability, ethnicity/racial group, sex/gender, sexuality and social group). Practitioners who challenge these processes take appropriate action against them.

Curriculum: although practitioners in primary schools who work with the National Curriculum may associate the word with the statutory programmes of study, in this framework the term is used in a different way. It refers to the whole sum of experiences, activities, interactions, and opportunities that are made available to young children - everything, in short, from which young children learn. All that young children see and hear and do, all that their educators do and say - and do not do or say - all of these experiences are part of the early years curriculum.

Early childhood practitioners: all those who work with other people's children under the age of eight.

Setting: early childhood practitioners work in a variety of settings, including all those listed on pages 6 and 7.

Section Two
The foundations for early learning

Introduction

This section introduces the **FOUNDATIONS for early learning**, from birth to the age of eight. From the foundations, **GOALS for early learning** have been developed: these are presented and illustrations from a variety of settings are given to show how these two elements of the framework can be used:

- to help practitioners see more clearly the quality of children's learning;
- to trace the continuity of children's learning from birth to eight;
- to recognise and value the diversity of practices in early childhood settings.

The foundations

Quality in Diversity, the framework as a whole, is based on the **FOUNDATIONS for early learning**. Working from their agreed principles, and drawing on *Te Whāriki*, the inspiring curriculum document from New Zealand (New Zealand Ministry of Education 1993), the member organisations of the Early Childhood Education Forum identified five key ideas that are integral to worthwhile learning in the early years. These key ideas are known as the **FOUNDATIONS for early learning**.

These five foundations are, essentially, shorthand descriptions of the whole range of young children's learning. Each of the five foundations is equally important. For consistency, they are presented throughout this document in a particular order, but this is not to suggest that one is more important than any other. Fuller descriptions of the foundations are given below.

BELONGING AND CONNECTING: from birth, young children are learning to form mutually respectful relationships with adults and other children in families, communities and group settings. They are learning to make choices about aspects of their identities as girls and boys and as members of ethnic/racial, linguistic, social, cultural (and religious) groups.

BEING AND BECOMING: from birth, young children are learning self-respect and feelings of self-worth and identity. They are learning to take care of themselves and to keep safe and well.

CONTRIBUTING AND PARTICIPATING: from birth, young children are learning to contribute and participate in families and other groups. They are learning to support each other, to care for each other, and to collaborate. They are learning to make choices and to understand how their choices affect others.

BEING ACTIVE AND EXPRESSING: from birth, young children are mentally and physically active, learning to act on the world, to try things out, to see what happens. They are learning to express their ideas, thoughts and feelings, alone and with others, in a variety of ways.

THINKING, IMAGINING AND UNDERSTANDING: from birth, young children begin to think in a variety of ways: wondering, imagining, puzzling, dreaming, asking questions. They are learning to understand themselves and the world around them. They are learning to think critically and in a balanced way.

The definitions of the **FOUNDATIONS** were the starting point for the development work of the *Quality in Diversity* project.

Goals for early learning

Members of the project worked together to expand the foundations into more detailed expressions of what the **FOUNDATIONS** stand for. The outcomes of this work have been called the **GOALS for early learning**. In the process of development, project members drew on their own accumulated experience in many different types of setting, and on the wisdom and experience of acknowledged authors and researchers in the world of early childhood.

**Belonging and connecting:
What do these words mean for children's learning?**

- forming mutually respectful relationships with close and familiar adults and children, through verbal and non-verbal communication (touch, movement, gestures, signs, dialects and languages)

- learning to recognise and accept the needs and rights of familiar adults and children

- learning how to communicate their own needs and rights, within their intimate groups (of children and adults)

- sympathising with the needs of other forms of life (plants and animals), treating them with respect and care

- learning to show respect for the natural and made environments to which they belong (early years setting, home and neighbourhood)

- learning about family history through the sounds, smells, tastes, stories and artifacts which represent continuity and change in their families and cultures

- learning about their membership of groups and the possibility of being, at times, dependent and independent, acquiescent and assertive, of leading and following, in peer groups, family and community

- learning about the groups (including ethnic/racial, cultural, linguistic, religious, social) to which familiar adults and children belong

- gradually learning about their membership of groups beyond their immediate surroundings (ethnic/racial, linguistic, cultural, social and religious)

- building on their first-hand experiences of belonging and connecting, coming to understand more about other people and other communities, past and present

belonging
and
connecting

Being and becoming:
What do these words mean for children's learning?

- being healthy, secure and safe from physical and emotional harm

- changing and developing at their own pace and in individual ways

- being proud of, enjoying and respecting their bodies, their gestures, their movements, including aspects of their ethnic/racial group, skin colour and other physical characteristics, sex/gender and special qualities, disabilities or aptitudes

- gaining self-respect and enjoyment from their achievements

- becoming individuals with personal interests, which they pursue independently and with others, in a variety of ways

- becoming aware of and making decisions about their own identities, and those of others, in all their differences and similarities (including sex/gender, ethnic/racial group, skin colour and other physical characteristics, cultures, languages and religions)

- becoming aware of negative stereotypes that can constrain individual development and achievement through discrimination

- being able to be assertive and learning to challenge stereotypes

- becoming confident learners

- becoming able to value and understand the variety of languages and cultures of the society in which we all live

- being and becoming a communicator of increasing skill and confidence (verbal and non-verbal, gestures, signs, dialects and languages)

- being and becoming more aware of written languages and aspects of literacy (stories and images, including those on a computer screen)

being
and
becoming

Contributing and participating:
What do these words mean for children's learning?

- participating in the life of the groups in which they live and learn, in play, in friendship, in negotiating and resolving conflict, in celebration and in sorrow

- collaborating in shared activities, with familiar adults and with children

- contributing their unique and individual thoughts, feelings, ideas and activities

- taking growing responsibility for themselves in the groups to which they belong

- learning to understand and reflect on the impact of their choices and decisions on others (adults and children)

- learning to understand and contribute to the shared customs and traditions of their homes and early childhood settings

- learning to take part in caring for familiar others (adults and children), for living things and for their environment

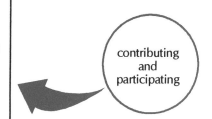

contributing and participating

Being active and expressing:
What do these words mean for children's learning?

- discovering, investigating and practising their mental and physical powers

- discovering and investigating and the world around them

- setting themselves problems and challenges

- expressing their ideas, feelings and emotional needs through a variety of forms (verbal and non-verbal, symbolic and imaginative play)

- representing their ideas and feelings through a variety of symbolic systems (paint, dance, music, rhythm, mathematical, spoken and sign languages)

- becoming critically aware of the world they live in, and asking questions about what puzzles and intrigues them

- learning to make up their own minds about what they are told and what they find out for themselves

being active and expressing

Thinking, imagining and understanding:
What do these words mean for children's learning?

- making sense of the world, as they meet it through their first-hand experiences and explore it through play

- testing out their ideas, looking for explanations, asking questions

- finding out from other people, from children, from books and other media, as they build on their own first-hand experiences

- exercising their imagination and creativity in a wide variety of activities and materials, indoors and outdoors, large scale and 'miniature world', alone and in collaboration with others

- reflecting on their experiences and those of others as they come to understand abstract concepts and moral dilemmas (eg fairness, justice, rejection)

- learning to think with empathy about the experiences of others, taking account of other people's perspectives, feelings and concerns

- finding out about and coming to understand their own cultural, linguistic, social and ethnic/racial backgrounds and those of others, recognising and valuing differences and similarities

- learning to think critically about the world, recognising and challenging prejudice, bias and discrimination

- learning to communicate their thinking and understanding in a variety of forms (spoken, written, non-verbal)

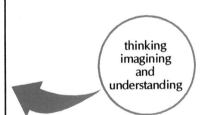

Foundations and goals for early learning: some illustrations

The following pages contain observations of young children learning contributed by members of the *Quality in Diversity* project. The observations were made of children from birth to eight in a range of different settings from right across the country, with a diversity of approaches. They are given here for two purposes: first, simply to illustrate what the **FOUNDATIONS** and **GOALS for early learning** look like in real life; and secondly, more importantly, to illustrate how these elements of the framework can be used as an evaluative tool with which practitioners can examine the *quality* of children's experiences, while maintaining the *diversity* in their practices that is an essential part of effective early childhood education today.

Example one

Belonging and connecting

Relevant goals	*Observation*
• forming mutually respectful relationships with familiar adults and children • treating plants and animals with respect and care • learning about their family culture and history • learning about their membership of the nursery group, family and wider community	*This observation was made one morning in a setting for children between three and four. Kobir, aged three and a half was brought from home by his grandmother, accompanied by little sister, Pria, aged two and a half.* *This was the first time the grandmother had visited the setting, and as they entered the building, Kobir hastened to show his grandmother the photographs taken on a recent visit to the local fire station. These photos were being displayed on the 'family notice board', which also had space for a number of notices giving information about the setting in the various languages represented in the local community.* *The practitioners warmly welcomed Pria (whom they already knew well) and her grandmother. They asked the children to introduce them, and if they would like to show their grandmother around. The children agreed, with pleasure, and started with the home corner, where Kobir made straight for the chappati board - 'like ours, but littler'. Next came the goldfish, and Kobir's turn to feed them. 'You do it', he said to Pria, 'then you'll know how, when you come to playschool'.*

Implications for *Quality in Diversity*

- The practitioners in this setting were proud of their 'family notice board' and the way they had made it a priority to use community languages in their notices and displays. They were pleased to see new visitors make use of this part of their provision.

- They wondered if there was more they could do to familiarise their children with the spoken forms of these languages. They agreed to contact the neighbouring provisions for young children to compare practice, and to see if they could learn from one another.

- The practitioners had recently reviewed their policy on visits outside the setting, and had decided to do more very local visits, to ordinary and everyday places and people, and fewer of the rather special events they had planned before (a day at the seaside, a trip to the theatre). They wondered if parents and other carers had understood the thinking behind this change, and decided to be more explicit about it, as well as involving families in suggesting and organising suitable 'mini-visits'. They were delighted when one child's grandmother suggested (one fine week in late September) that a small group of children could come and help her collect the windfalls from her old apple tree.

- The practitioners discussed the possibility of deliberately increasing the number of family visitors to their provision, and not just leaving it to chance. They wanted all their children to have the experience of their family members being welcomed and shown around, being made to feel part of the wider community of which the setting was a part.

Example two

Being and becoming

Relevant goals	*Observation*
• being healthy, secure and safe • enjoying their bodies and their movements • becoming individuals with personal interests • being and becoming communicators of increasing skill and confidence	*This observation was made in a setting that included provision for under-threes. The focus of the observation was Angelina (31 months). Extracts from the observer's notes are given below.* *Angelina is now playing on her own and has reclaimed a sit and ride toy. She bangs it down near Sonya; she trips herself off it; she falls on the floor; she begins to cry. J (her key person) comes to her; she holds her and comforts her; picks her up and walks with her around the end of the garden stroking her and talking with her gently. J now lifts her up even higher, so that they can both look over the wall of the garden together. They turn together and wave to some of the children who are watching and playing at that end of the garden, but J continues to hold Angelina.* *They look over at the mothers and babies who are in the park on the other side of the wall. I cannot hear what the conversation is about, but I can see that they are talking with each other. I can see by J's gestures and Angelina's responses that now they are talking about the leaves blowing off the trees at the end of the garden. Angelina and J are still together and Angelina is running at the end of the playground and excitedly watching the leaves spin down from the tree to the ground as the wind blows them off the branches. J has at last found an activity which matches Angelina's need for action and her interest. J offers her sustained and individual attention at the bottom of the garden. Angelina is having a very enjoyable, animated and exciting time catching the spinning leaves one by one. After catching each leaf she runs back to J to be lifted up with her, and look again over the wall.* *J holds her lovingly and they watch the other children together. Angelina seems calmer and snuggles into her and watches the children over the other side of the wall sleepily. She seems to be more relaxed than I have seen her before.*

Angelina is floppy and relaxed and J is holding her and stroking her back affectionately. She seems happy just to lie against her body now, even though J is now talking with other adults. Even so she is still holding Angelina and carrying her around with her, and Angelina seems secure there. For six minutes I note she is limp and sleepy and calm and floppy and seems content to hear the adults talking to one another. I have timed it but it seems so much longer than six minutes, it is such a relief and a pleasure to observe this calm episode after all the earlier frantic agitation. Then J places her down on the ground again. As soon as Angelina is separated physically from J by being put on the ground she resumes her whizzing behaviour. She whizzes round and round and round and J says to her 'Angelina you will get all dizzy'. Angelina comes running back to be gathered up in J's arms again.

Implications for *Quality in Diversity*

- When Angelina hurt herself physically, J, her key person, attended to her in a way that seemed to 'hold' her physical pain; she didn't make light of the hurt or dismiss Angelina after a quick cuddle. J also seemed to 'hold' Angelina's emotional pain, her frantic agitation. Angelina's relief (and the observer's) was evident.

- Within the security of her relationship with J, Angelina was able to allow her body to move in synchrony with the spinning leaves; as they spun around, floating and changing direction, so did she. And as she caught each leaf she, too, turned back to J to be 'caught'. J seemed to be positively confirming Angelina's bodily gestures, and her closeness with the leaves.

- J supported Angelina's interest in the leaves, and in the mothers and babies in the part on the other side of the wall. She gave both physical support (so that Angelina could see over the wall) and emotional support, as Angelina watched the mothers and babies together, outside the setting, with all the difficult feelings this might start up in her.

- Angelina and J were engaged together in a rich mixture of communication - verbal and non verbal, conscious and unconscious. J seemed to be helping Angelina to understand that being frantic was not inescapable, or inevitable, but something that J can contain, and that Angelina will, in turn, become able to contain too.

Example three

Contributing and participating

Relevant goals	*Observation*
• participating in the life of the group • collaborating with familiar children • learning to take their part in caring for each other • taking growing responsibility for themselves	*In a setting for children from the age of two and a half, the children gathered together in small groups in the middle of the afternoon for a snack - yogurt, jelly and juice. The older children kept the small tables supplied with dishes, spoons and beakers, and all the children took responsibility for clearing away their places when they had eaten and drunk together. The two practitioners took little part in managing this relaxed and welcoming period of refreshment: the children were very much in control.* *Max, two-years-old, and just out of nappies, was observed as he stood at the sink washing his bowl. He knew exactly what to do and was confident in following the routine he had been taught: 'dip, drip and dry'. He dipped his bowl in the warm soapy water, in and out, two or three times, held it in the air above the sink while the excess water dripped away, and then used the cloth laid beside the sink to dry the bowl. Unfortunately, in the middle of this familiar sequence of actions, his bladder control let him down, and Max looked away from the sink to see a stream of urine running down his legs on to the tiled floor. His expression changed; first, an anxious, distressed frown, then, as he caught the eye of one of the practitioners who was sitting nearby smiling at him warmly, a cheerful grin. He put his bowl back in the sink, but before he could go any further, a three-and-a-half-year-old friend of his appeared with a child-sized floor mop. She held it out to Max who took it and dealt with the puddle on the ground. While he put the mop away, the elder child finished washing and drying Max's beaker and spoon.*

Implications for *Quality in Diversity*

- The practitioners had set up an informal and relaxed snack time in order to create opportunities for children just to be together, for social exchanges around the table, time for children to participate in the life of the group.

- The routines of setting the tables and clearing away were carefully taught so that even the youngest children were confident in exercising responsibility for looking after themselves.

- The observation shows how much more than this the children seem to be learning; besides care of self, they were learning care of each other; besides contributing to the social exchanges at the table, children were learning to contribute to the good of the whole group.

- Not all practitioners would expect such young children to take on these responsibilities. In other settings, children's experiences of contributing and participating might take different forms, and the physical care of the environment would be the adult practitioners' responsibility.

Example four

Being active and expressing

Relevant goals	*Observation*
• discovering and practising their mental and physical powers • discovering and investigating themselves and the world around them • setting themselves problems and challenges • representing their ideas in a variety of ways • asking questions about what puzzles and intrigues them • learning to make up their own minds about what they are told and what they find out for themselves	*In a small room with access to a covered outdoor area, a group of four-year-olds was observed playing at 'barges', an interest stimulated by a familiar children's television programme. The practitioners and parents had noticed this theme developing in their play, and had added to their regular provision some milk crates, some guttering, and large cardboard boxes.* *The four children set themselves the task of roping the milk crates (barges) together in one long line. They discussed who would haul the barges and who would be in charge of the individual vessels in the chain. Three children leapt into the crates and the fourth began to haul - but the knots all came undone. Time to think again: much rearrangement of the crates, lively discussion, many experiments with different knots, and another trial took place. This time the knots held but the load was too heavy for the child with the rope. She called for help, and two children nearby came to join her, while they all started to sing the song which introduces the television programme.*

Implications for *Quality in Diversity*

- The practitioners in this example were aware that the small classroom in which they worked offered children few opportunities for physical activity on a large scale. They had decided earlier to open up the outdoor area, and to include it in their overview of provision for play and first hand experience; this observation was welcome evidence that this 'outdoor classroom', as they thought of it, was being well-used.

- However, they were still not satisfied that the space provided was sufficient for all the children to have enough opportunities for large scale physical activity. They decided to monitor their use of timetabled sessions in their large hall, to see if they could bring this part of the programme more into line with these particular **goals for early learning**.

- They noticed how much information about the world the children had acquired from the television programme, and asked themselves whether the children had access to enough factual information books, and whether they, the practitioners, could do more to encourage future exploration and enquiry through imaginative and physical play.

- Having made notes of this play sequence and its successes and failures, the practitioners decided to use it as part of their weekly review with all the children of the activities that had been most rewarding and challenging. They decided they would try to encourage the children who had not been involved in the play to ask questions and to make comments about various aspects of the play, and the original television programme. What else might children want to know about ropes? And knots? What else was there to learn? What other connections might be made? These would all be good questions to explore with the children.

Example five

Thinking, imagining and understanding

Relevant goals	*Observation*
• making sense of the world • testing out ideas, looking for explanations • finding out from other people and from books • learning to think with empathy about the experiences of others • finding out about the historical and cultural backgrounds of others • learning to think critically about the world	*This observation was made in a Y3 classroom with 32 children aged from seven to eight. They were studying* The Victorians *as part of the history component of the National Curriculum. In the course of their library work two children, Helen and Natalie, came across the name of Mary Seacole, a black nurse who travelled from Jamaica to the Crimea to work as a nurse at the front line. They decided to investigate further but soon discovered that very few books in the school library so much as mentioned Mary Seacole. They considered possible reasons for this omission during a class discussion. After a visit to the local library, Helen and Natalie embarked on their own biography of Mary Seacole to put in the school library, 'so that other children won't be ignorant about her'. Natalie's mother had also become interested and commented: 'I didn't even know about her and I'm from Jamaica - we didn't learn about such things in school'.* *When the book was finished, the girls asked if they could make 'a sort of risks game'. They designed and made a board game, using their knowledge of Seacole's life and dramatic journeys to create 'hazard' and 'fortitude' cards. Helen had found the words fortitude and hazard in one of Mary Seacole's letters and had asked what they meant. They wrote on one 'hazard' card: 'When Mary Seacole came to London people were prejudiced against her because of her colour. She couldn't get a job as a nurse. GO BACK 6 SPACES'. They wrote on a 'fortitude' card: 'Mary Seacole was very kind and determined. She wanted to help the poor soldiers so she paid for herself to go to the Crimea. ADVANCE 10 SPACES'.* *Later in the term when the children were writing self-portraits for their school achievement profiles Natalie reflected 'I would like to be like Mary Seacole'.*

Implications for *Quality in Diversity*

- When the teachers who worked with this group of children reviewed the topic, as it drew to a close, they noted many examples of significant learning and important kinds of thinking (as shown in *Relevant goals*, above).

- They also noted how great a part reading and writing had played in this topic, and asked themselves whether they could have built in more opportunities for other forms of representation and communication (spoken, musical, pictorial, dramatic).

- They wondered if they could have taken the children's thinking further in terms of abstract concepts; they noted Helen's and Natalie's confident use of words such as prejudice, hazard and fortitude, and put together a list of other 'keywords' that could have been explored in the course of the topic (rejection, courage, justice and injustice).

- They discussed the possibility that in their next historical topic, they could do more to encourage children's critical thinking about books and other resources. They recognised the danger of children relying too readily on the accuracy of textbooks and information books.

Conclusion

This section introduced the **FOUNDATIONS** and **GOALS for early learning**. Five illustrative examples were given to demonstrate how these elements of the framework can be used to evaluate the quality of children's experiences. The examples were taken from brief observations, carried out by practitioners in the course of their daily practice, and show how even such short periods of observation can offer valuable evidence about children's learning, and about the ways in which practitioners support and extend that learning.

Section Three
Learning, play and children's entitlements

Introduction

The **FOUNDATIONS** and **GOALS** for early learning, described in detail in Section Two, were developed by the members of the *Quality in Diversity* project, drawing on their accumulated knowledge and understanding of how young children learn. This understanding is based both on first hand experiences of working with young children, and on the work of the great educators of the past who have informed and inspired the early years community.

In this section, the **FOUNDATIONS** are used to:

- identify some of the most important characteristics of young children's learning that change and develop from birth to eight

- demonstrate the importance of play in young children's learning

- describe the conditions that are essential for early learning, that is, the entitlements that must be met to ensure children's learning is supported and extended.

Learning from birth to eight

We know that children's learning during their first eight years of life has many characteristics that are common right across the age range. We also know that there are many differences between a new-born baby, a toddler of two and a child of seven. Some of the most important of these differences are summarised below. There are many good books describinge stages and phases of children's development from birth to eight years more fully (for example Lindon 1993); some suggestions for further reading are given in Appendix 3.

Early learning: children under three

Babies quickly learn where they belong, from the sensations, sounds and smells that surround them at home. They learn to recognise the people who care for them, who hold them and carry them about. They learn their mother's milky smell, the strength of their grandfather's hands, the touch of their grandmother's curls, the rhythm of their father's walk, the sounds of talking and music in the home.

Alongside and building on this sense of belonging to the close family circle, babies and young children begin to learn about other people - the extended family, the childminder, the practitioners in their preschool settings.

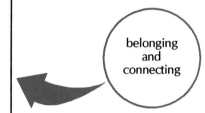

From birth, children are learning about themselves. Their first task is to learn what is 'me' and what is 'not me'. While in the womb, they have been continually held and safely contained by their mothers. Now they must learn that they are separate beings: they must learn where their being ends and others begin. As they do so, they seek a continued sense of secure containment.

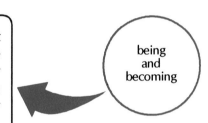

Babies are born with the desire to communicate and to understand the whole repertoire of intonations, facial expressions, bodily movements, mannerisms and games of the adults who care for them. They are learning all the time to tune into the conversations going on around them, to use their smiles, coos and babbles in conversational exchanges with adults who are ready to tune into them, and their contributions.

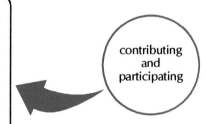

As part of their new separateness, babies are learning about intense feelings inside themselves, including anxiety, fear and rage. They need much comforting and holding to help them cope with these feelings, which can easily seem overwhelming.

But they are also learning that, although separate, they are not alone. They learn about feelings of happiness and love for others. They learn that people and things who disappear can also reappear; the hiding games that their carers play with them help them to understand that loving and beloved adults who have to leave them will also return.

At the same time, babies are learning to explore the world, and themselves, through their physical activity. They are learning about the different parts of their bodies and how to control them. They are learning to represent their experiences in expressive movement.

They seem to have a burning desire to be mobile, to see more of the exciting world around them. They persevere until they can lift their heads, they practise rolling over, they persist with crawling until they can control direction and speed; they progress to confident walking, running and climbing. Inevitably, sometimes they will attempt too much, and fall over and be bitterly upset. They may be physically bruised and they may also be humiliated by what feels like failure. Nevertheless, their growing physical control opens up the possibility of self-reliance and independence.

being
active
and
expressing

At first, babies' thinking is in the present, the here and now. Watching, listening, smelling, mouthing and tasting, touching - all their senses and sensations are food for thought and growing understanding.

Once children are confident walkers, their hands are free to explore more of the world around them, and to find out how it works. They learn about their own capacity to act on the world, to push and pull, twist and turn, to lift, carry and drop, to tip and pour. They are learning how things and people respond to their actions, as they investigate 'what happens if . . .?' and 'what can I do with this?'

Their interest in the adults around them leads them into imitative and symbolic play, as they represent their experiences, ideas and feelings in imaginative play, where one thing can stand for another (an empty carton for a cup of tea, a banana for a telephone).

thinking
imagining
and
understanding

Early learning: children from three to five

Children learn to belong and connect in their relationships as they explore the possibilities of life in groups. These groups - their family at home, groups in the neighbourhood, early childhood settings - provide scripts, costumes and scenery for increasingly complex and dramatic play. Outdoors and in, in private places and in the domestic play area, children play out the patterns and predicaments of their relationships.

They use all manner of materials: gaudy plastic play things, natural wood and stone, traditional blocks, and popular video stars. Preparing real food for the family meals and festivals, and cooking pretend feasts for their imaginary adventures are all part of learning to connect with friends and groups of friends.

Children learn, too, about the constraints and difficulties of joining in; they experience the pain of rejection. In their friendship groups, they practise the art of leadership and of being led; they learn coping strategies for managing teasing and disappointment. They are also beginning to value each other's different family and social codes of kindness and etiquette, and about the subtleties of relationships in different community groups, however big or small.

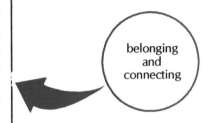

These children are learning to be independent beings within the security of relationships with key people in their nursery groups and with their close adults at home. They are learning about choices and boundaries, the possibilities of their gender and cultural identities. They learn who they are as they run and chase and experiment in their play. They try on the adult roles of paid work and home management. They learn to manage their own toilet needs, dressing, eating, and all the other tasks of caring for their bodies, their health and well-being.

In all this, children are being and becoming their unique selves, with particular attributes, capabilities, personal flair, and distinctive beauty. They learn to accept their own frailties, beastliness, and vulnerability as they play the part of the dog who is patted, or the baby who is soothed with a doody and tucked into bed. As they learn more about themselves, and who they might become, they are learning about universal human qualities, as well as about the differences between people.

learning that they can make significant
social relationships. In their play, they act
depends on absolute fairness. They are
ish the rules of fairness, making a case and
creasing confidence and fluency. They are
nd to comply with the conventions of the
ate in they are learning to apologise, to
ook after one another. They experience
frustration in these endeavours, and are
and reasons why. They are learning about
een democracy and dictatorship, between
otism, between furious frustration and
between quarrelling and making amends.

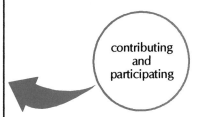

arning to express themselves in a variety of
and movement, and through the symbolic
t, music and spoken languages. They are
ell as passing feelings. They gradually learn
oderate their expressions of rage and
contain their excitement, or urgent need for
to the conventions of the nursery, family
y group. But they are still spontaneous and
ssing their feelings - about separations and
le

is opening new doors and windows on the
works. For example, they explore the
on paper, with dabs, lines and curves; they
nd space with toy trucks and tricycles; they
e and symmetry as they handle bricks and
bout sound and rhythm as they experiment
heir bodies, with musical instruments and
They learn to use simple tools (scissors,
ith increasing dexterity and purpose.

arning to understand a wide variety of issues
and ideas. Their thinking is becoming, at times, scientific,
technological, moral and creative, as they pursue their interests
and concerns. They are learning to form hypotheses and try out
ideas about the world and the people in it, investigating the Why?
and How? and What? questions that puzzle and intrigue them.
They respond actively to the stories they are told, and transform
them into their imaginative play, as they learn about the world
through narrative, myth, fairy story and fiction.

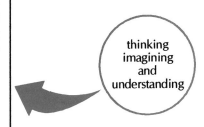

Early learning: children from five to eight

These children are reaching out beyond their intimate and familiar surroundings into the wider world; they are learning as members of different communities, cultural, religious and linguistic groups. They are moving beyond an overwhelming interest in the here and now, the present and particular; they can see how they too are part of their family's history, and how they are connected together through the traditions of their communities.

They join with adults in community work, worship and celebrations: they play in the carnival steel band, for example, they pray and make offerings in the temple, they work to clear the village churchyard of bracken, they build a bonfire.

These children make connections in their friendship groups through an exploration of shared languages, dialects, jokes, and slang; they are fluent in their family and community languages, and in the humour and wit of the street, the playground and their private games.

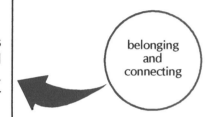

belonging and connecting

These children are learning about their physical strengths, capabilities, personal style and appearance. They are preoccupied with their identity in their friendship groups, their gangs and clubs, and their need to imitate and conform. This preoccupation is an important step on the way to establishing a secure identity, and confidence in being one's own unique self in the midst of others. Hairstyles, dress codes, buzzwords, fads and fashions are the symbols of being and becoming in these children's lives.

They are becoming aware of their own intellectual and physical powers, which are considerable. They are essentially meaning makers - making sense of the world through talk. They use spoken languages for a variety of purposes: to get things done, and make things happen, to describe, to question, to wonder, to guess, to justify, to complain and critically evaluate. They can hold long purposeful conversations. They can develop rich imaginative play sequences. They can express their personal opinions and defend their views.

being and becoming

Early Childhood Education Forum

These children are willing collaborators: in play, in problem-solving and in group projects. They are developing working ideas of justice and fairness, and are coming to understand the importance of listening to different points of view. They are becoming increasingly independent: responsibly looking after themselves in many ways, and learning to take care of others too. They are learning what it means to be trusted and to consider the implications of the choices and decisions they make.

These children often choose to be part of groups of the same sex or skin colour, or with a common interest. As they experience the security of these groups, and feel their contributions valued, they develop the confidence to challenge stereotypes. They dare to be different themselves and to respect the different contributions of other children, other groups.

contributing
and
participating

These children are physically skilful: they can be expressive dancers, join in skipping and ball games, ride wheeled toys, climb rocks and trees, use fine paint brushes, play musical instruments, play games with pebbles and seeds, use needles and thread and manipulate computer mice. Some children can swim, dive, or roller skate.

They are emotionally active too, willing and able to express their feelings. They can feel empathy and compassion for others and reflect on the emotional impact of everyday events. They can understand and express sorrow and joy, hope and anxiety.

being
active
and
expressing

These children lead energetic intellectual lives, in their homes, schools and play spaces; they are powerful thinkers, imaginative, enquiring, logical and fantastic. They are amassing understanding about a huge variety of topics: for example, size, shape, numbers and weight, colour, light and beauty, life and death, plants and animals, right and wrong, rules, routines and expectations, joy and sorrow, safety and danger, energy, time and the concept of mind.

These children are learning to use the resources of their expanding world to take up their places as artists, performers, technicians, administrators, researchers and philosophers.

thinking
imagining
and
understanding

The importance of play

Children's learning, from birth to eight, is enthralling in its diversity. Yet running through the descriptions given above is one single strand that is of crucial importance for practitioners trying to understand the complexity of learning: it is the fundamental principle that children learn through play. Play is essential for the healthy growth and successful development of young human beings. Play is central to all young children's learning, from babies in the first few months of life, through to children of statutory school age and beyond.

One of the Early Childhood Education Forum principles states:

> *Young children learn best through play, first-hand experience and talk.*

In this statement of principle, the member organisations of ECEF are not alone.

- *Purposeful play is an essential and rich part of the learning process. Play is a powerful motivator, encouraging children to be creative and to develop their ideas, understanding and language. Through play, children explore, apply and test out what they know.*
  Starting with Quality (The Rumbold Report) DES 1990

- *Purposeful play features strongly in good pre-school education.*
  The Education of Children Under Five DES/HMI 1989

- *The education of young children is founded in play.*
  Better Schools DES/Welsh Office 1985

How do these important insights connect with the ideas represented in this framework? What can the foundations and goals for early learning tell us about play that we don't already know?

In the following pages, we will see how the framework can:

- show us the richness and the value of the learning that takes place when children from birth to eight are engaged in sustained, purposeful play

- give us a shared vocabulary and conceptual map with which to describe that learning

- help us to ensure that what children of different ages learn through their play is in tune with our aspirations for them, both before and after they reach statutory school age

- demonstrate how the play of children who are following the National Curriculum programmes of study is rich in opportunities for learning.

The following examples of children's play illustrate each of the foundations and one of its associated goals for children's learning.

Children's play and the foundations for early learning

In their play, children are learning about each other, and about how people live, work and play together, in their families and communities. They are exploring cultural differences. They are learning about different kinds of relationships, which they repeat, renew and recreate in their imaginative play.

belonging and connecting

In their play children are learning about themselves, about who they are and what they might become. They experiment with what they can do, without fear of failure. They develop confidence, a sense of self-worth and identity. They make and break their own rules. They try out different roles, and explore and challenge stereotypes. They learn to communicate with increasing skill and confidence.

being and becoming

In their play, children are learning to take risks and be responsible for their actions. In cooperative play, they begin to accept responsibility for others. They learn to persevere, and gain satisfaction from joining with others.

contributing and participating

In their play, children explore and transform their worlds. They talk about their discoveries, sharing them with children and adults. They are learning to act like scientists, artists and musicians, curiously trying out new possibilities, finding new ways of expressing their ideas and their interests, their identities and their membership of diverse family and cultural groups.

being active and expressing

In their play, children use their imagination to explore ideas and feelings. They are learning to make sense of their own experiences, and to learn from the experiences of others. In their play, children puzzle and dream, create stories and imaginary worlds. They have space and time to wonder at the world about them, and to struggle with and reflect on deep feelings and challenging ideas. They develop a sense of fairness and justice.

thinking imagining and understanding

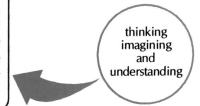

Belonging and connecting in play

Some illustrations of one of the goals for children's learning

Forming mutually respectful relationships with close and familiar adults and children through verbal and non-verbal communication

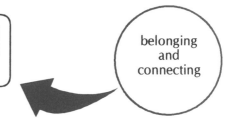

belonging
and
connecting

Children under three

- *Angus (24 months) has learned to participate in the settling to sleep procedure in his preschool setting, as the practitioners gently rub the children's backs and stroke their eyelids. Angus was observed in the home corner, re-enacting this ritual with the dolls, patting their backs and rubbing their eyelids until they too fell asleep.*

- *Noor (28 months) joined Jack at the water tray and together they developed a game of making the water flow out over one of the ledges in the moulded tray. They discovered how to increase and decrease the volume and velocity of the water, and accompanied their play with conversational exchanges and splashy (non-verbal) sound effects.*

Children from three to five

- *Jessica played at being a bride, after she had attended a wedding. She selected her bridesmaids from among her friends, staying in role while she instructed them what to do. She made the wedding food out of plasticine and Play-Doh, with the help of her friends.*

- *Euan was playing with the big blocks near the domestic play area. He stumbled and cracked his shins across one of the blocks. He was so distressed that all the children nearby stopped their play and came to investigate. Daniel knelt down and stroked Euan's legs for a moment and then leapt to his feet again. 'I know, I'll phone your mum!' He disappeared into the 'house' and emerged with a shiny black purse which he was using as a mobile phone. 'Here's your mum, you talk to her, Euan'.*

Children from five to eight

- *Two five-year-olds worked together with the wooden building blocks to make a construction to house a collection of toy cars and aeroplanes. They made a complicated long, narrow building with towers, ramps and staircases, and each took responsibility for one end of it. By watching each other attentively, and with frequent visits to check on each other's progress, they achieved a finished product which was perfectly symmetrical.*

Being and becoming in play

Some illustrations of one of the goals for children's learning

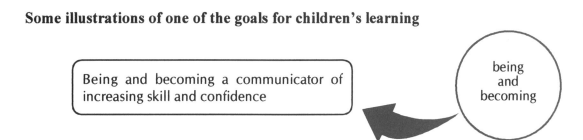

Being and becoming a communicator of increasing skill and confidence

being and becoming

Children under three

- *Three babies between seven and nine months were seated around a large 'Treasure Basket'. Silas picked out the metal tea-strainer and the metal sieve and leaned over towards Christopher, offering the objects to him. Christopher paused for a moment, put down the brush he was holding, and accepted Silas' offer. Silas did not let go of the objects till Christopher had a good grip; then Christopher offered them back to him, Silas chortled and accepted; this conversation-like exchange went on for three more turns.*

Children from three to five

- *Eleanor used the puppets to retell the story she had listened to on the previous day. She remembered the sequence of events, and many of the exact expressions used by the princess (her favourite puppet).*

- *A group of Traveller children were playing in a playvan organised by the local under eights adviser. Two children were using a wooden lorry and trailer/caravan, and piled all the furniture from the dolls houses into the trailer in a heap. The playworker said: 'Oh look, the people can't get in now, it's such a mess. Shall we sort the furniture out and tidy it up?' One child strongly objected: 'No! We're pulling away. (This means 'leaving the site' - observer's note). We always pile things in when we pull away; we don't go in the trailer, we go in the motor' (lorry). The playworkers later found out that eviction notices had just been served (not for the first time) on these children's families.*

Children from five to eight

- *Three six-year-olds, gripped by a craze for dinosaurs, built a miniature dinosaur world, using a children's encyclopaedia as a reference point. They used a variety of materials to create the background for their models, and played out long and complicated stories. At first they spoke spontaneously, but then they decided to record their stories on audio-cassettes, listening, checking and re-recording till every detail was as they wished it. They lent their tapes to other children so that they too could join in the dinosaur dramatic play.*

Contributing and participating in play

Some illustrations of one of the goals for children's learning

> Collaborating in shared activities, with familiar adults and with children

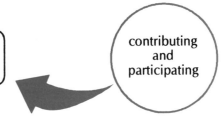

contributing and participating

Children under three

- *Archie (25 months) was sitting on his keyworker's lap having just woken from his afternoon nap. He picked up a yellow sticklebrick and held it up saying 'It's a blue one'. J replied 'It's a **yellow** one'. Archie made his sticklebrick into a candle by sticking another short piece in the end to represent the flame and pushed the whole candle on to a large flat base (the cake). J said 'Ooh, look at that cake - put another candle on'. Archie complied and then blew out the candles with a mighty puff.*

Children from three to five

- *Two children built an imaginary bus out of a large cardboard box, with improvised tyres, windows, seats, steering wheel and engine. Diana desperately wanted to be the bus driver and so did Alex. For a while they reasoned with each other; eventually Diana prevailed and the imaginative play began. Alex did not leave, but stayed in the role of passenger for a long time, suggesting new routes and exciting detours.*

- *Three children played on the climbing frame outdoors. They wore firefighters' hats and used pieces of rope as hoses. They shouted instructions to one another about the need to get everyone out of the house. One child pretended to be dead and was dragged from the scene. Another child pretended to give him an injection, and he returned to the play enthusiastically.*

Children from five to eight

- *In a large first school, Johnny (a six-year-old boy with a chronic and debilitating heart condition) was due to go into hospital for major surgery. The Y3 children at the top of this school organised a 'good luck assembly' for him, in great secrecy. They discussed a range of possibilities before deciding on a dramatic performance of one of Johnny's favourite stories. They created all the necessary props, costumes and dialogue, and rehearsed the whole piece in the classroom many times with great relish, much laughter and excitement.*

Being active and expressing in play

Some illustrations of one of the goals for children's learning

Discovering and investigating themselves and the world around them

being active and expressing

Children under three

● *Fergus (four months) was sitting on the sofa with his childminder, sucking contentedly on his bottle. He rubbed his toes up and down her legs, and then played with the hem of her skirt with his toes. He played with the front of her jumper with his right hand, squeezing, grasping, pulling, letting go, and then tried the same actions on her bare forearm. She squeaked at the ticklish feeling, and Fergus looked surprised. He turned his attention back to his toes, burying them in the soft sofa cushion before rubbing them on her legs again, seeming to enjoy the sensory variety all around him.*

Children from three to five

● *Over the weekend, a boy had been taken to see some dolphins, which had made a great impression on him. On Monday morning he walked into his preschool setting and fetched himself a long length of blue cloth, which he stretched out on the floor. He lay down on the cloth, on his belly, and crossed his ankles, moving his legs as he had seen the dolphins move their tails.*

● *A professional cellist visited a preschool setting to play and to talk about her instrument. After her visit, Zoe sat down on a low chair with one of the big wooden building blocks, which she held upright with her left hand. Then, with her right hand, she used a long piece of dowelling, in an exact imitation of the cellist's bow.*

Children from five to eight

● *A group of six-year-olds studied 'the Victorians'. The teacher converted the imaginative play area into a traditional elementary classroom, and a local grandparent came to talk about his memories of his early schooling before the First World War. After this visit, the children used the classroom scene to recreate the stories he had told, with many imaginative embellishments of their own. They were scrupulous in arranging that each child should play both teacher and pupil in turn.*

Thinking, imagining and understanding in play

Some illustrations of one of the goals for children's learning

Making sense of the world and exploring it through play

thinking
imagining
and
understanding

Children under three

● *Joanne (23 months) climbed on to A's lap (her keyworker) and fixed two sticklebricks together. J: 'My lollipop!'. A: 'Is it banana flavour?'. They pretended to lick it together. J (with a wicked smile) 'No, it's poo flavour!'. A: 'Ah, that's not nice . . .'* *Joanne reached for two more bricks and repeated the action of 'making a lollipop', then offered it to A once more. A: 'Ah **this** is the banana flavour? Very, very juicy'. Joanne squealed with conspirational glee.*

● *Samson (7 months) spent much of the observation period choosing to play with wheels. He twirled the dials on an activity centre, he rolled a truck on the floor. He watched the older children intently as they whizzed by on the sit-and-ride wheeled toys.*

Children from three to five

● *Jamil had made a model crocodile out of an egg box, and a group of children was pretending that the crocodile was frightening them. Jamil opened and closed the crocodile's mouth, making roaring sounds. He told them 'I'm a fierce crocodile'. The gleeful children after a while asked him to stop but he said that it was all right, as this crocodile had no teeth. The children then examined the crocodile's mouth and decided that it was safe; they started to stroke the animal which had so recently terrorised them. 'Did he used to have teeth?' asked one child. 'When he lived with his mummy, but now he's very old and he hasn't any' answered Jamil (the crocodile expert).*

Children from five to eight

● *Children who had taken part in the Notting Hill carnival came back to school full of enthusiasm. With their teachers they planned a 'school carnival'; they wrote a play and created masks, music and dances for it. In their planning for this topic, the teachers drew on the programmes of study for PE, art, music, English and design technology, as well as cross-curricular themes and dimensions.*

Children's entitlements

However much we know and understand about children's play and children's learning, our knowledge and understanding are not enough. Worthwhile learning in the early years does not come about by wishing for it.

Our commitment to quality, however passionately expressed, does not of itself bring it about. In the remaining pages of this section, we begin to examine the ways in which practitioners can turn their aspirations for children's learning into a living reality.

This part of the framework is structured around the concept of entitlement. The members of the *Quality in Diversity* project who developed the framework used the Foundations and Goals for early learning to establish **children's entitlements**; they asked themselves what conditions will ensure that the foundations for early learning are firmly established, for every child, in every different setting.

These entitlements, set out below, constitute a concise summary of how practitioners can make sure they play their part in building secure foundations for early learning. A more detailed discussion of the tasks and responsibilities of early years practitioners follows in Section Four.

Entitlements for all children

Children are entitled to
be cared for by a small number of familiar and consistent practitioners who understand and are sympathetic to their needs

and to be supported in their learning by practitioners who
work with parents/carers or other family members in a partnership of trust, respecting each other's concerns, circumstances, practices and traditions.

Children are entitled to
opportunities to form mutually respectful relationships with a range of other people, families and communities

and to be supported in their learning by practitioners who
act respectfully and with equal concern towards all the members of the community in which they work.

belonging
and
connecting

Children are entitled to
be well-fed, rested, physically active and mentally stimulated, safe from emotional and physical harm

and to be supported in their learning by practitioners who
are respectful of differences between individual children and who provide an environment, indoors and outdoors, that is healthy, interesting, involving, safe and enjoyable.

Children are entitled to
a sense of well-being, to feelings of self-worth and identity, and confidence in themselves as learners

and to be supported in their learning by practitioners who
have high expectations of all children's developing capabilities, giving them opportunities to take risks, to experience success and failure, and to reflect on their learning and achievement.

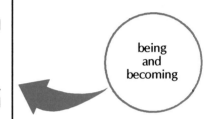

being and becoming

Children are entitled to
contribute their individual and unique thoughts, feelings and ideas, and to be respected for the choices and decisions they make

and to be supported in their learning by practitioners who
value them for their religious, ethnic/racial, cultural, linguistic and sex/gender identities, and for their special needs, aptitudes and interests.

Children are entitled to
opportunities to take on a range of responsibilities in the setting, progressively becoming more aware of what is involved in being a member of a group

and to be supported in their learning by practitioners who
welcome their contributions to shared endeavours, and to the tasks of caring for others, and who sensitively extend the range of each child's responsibilities.

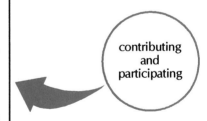

contributing and participating

Children are entitled to
opportunities to learn through their senses and physical activity, through active involvement in first hand experiences and play

and to be supported in their learning by practitioners who
plan and organise an environment, indoors and outdoors, for active learning, physical movement, first hand experiences, creativity and play.

Children are entitled to
express their feelings and emotional needs

and to be supported in their learning by practitioners who
are well-informed, sensitive and responsive to children's feelings and the full range of their emotional needs.

being active and expressing

Children are entitled to
opportunities to think, to understand, to ask questions, to learn skills and processes, and to pursue their own interests and concerns

and to be supported in their learning by practitioners who
listen, watch, take time to understand, welcome children's curiosity, follow where children lead, and provide time, space and opportunities for extending children's thinking, imagining and understanding.

Children are entitled to
opportunities to learn about themselves and others, to become critically aware, and to grow to recognise and challenge bias, stereotypes and discriminatory behaviour

and to be supported in their learning by practitioners who
treat everyone with respect and equal concern, who are committed to challenging prejudice and bias and who are aware of strategies for counteracting all forms of discrimination.

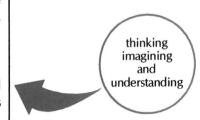

thinking imagining and understanding

Conclusion

In this section, the foundations and goals for early learning have been used to review some of what we already know about young children's learning, and about the importance of play in that learning. But it is not enough to consider learning without examining the practitioner's role; in the next section we move on from considering children's entitlements to a fuller examination of what practitioners do in fulfilling their responsibilities.

Section Four
The practitioner's part in early learning

Introduction

In this section, the **FOUNDATIONS** and **GOALS for early learning** are used to support an extended exploration of the part that practitioners play in children's learning, with a strong emphasis on the principle of partnership with parents and families. The central tasks of early years practitioners are discussed and illustrated, using examples contributed by members of the *Quality in Diversity* project. These examples demonstrate how the framework can be used to:

- monitor the quality of practice in early years settings
- focus attention on particular aspects of the practitioner's responsibilities
- raise questions about areas of provision that may need development.

What practitioners do

Most early years practitioners, at least some of the time, feel hurried and harassed, as if there were not enough hours in the day, or days in the week, to do all the dozens of different tasks they have set themselves, or to meet all their different responsibilities. They tend to think of themselves as busy people, with an ever-growing and endless list of what needs doing. And yet, for all the apparent pressure to keep busy, the central tasks of the practitioner can be very simply described.

All early years practitioners, in every kind of setting, however diverse these may be, take on certain inescapable commitments:

- **To plan** for children's learning.
- **To resource and organise** opportunities for their learning.
- **To support and extend** that learning.
- **To understand** what is happening as children learn.
- **To record progress** in children's learning.
- **To evaluate and adapt** what they do in the interests of children's learning.
- **To work in partnership** with parents, carers, other family members and colleagues.

This list of commitments is incomplete, however, without one essential further task; that is

● **To observe** children's learning.

It is only by observing children, as they live and learn, that we can be sure of having good enough information on which to act as we meet our responsibilities. We cannot support or extend learning without observing what children are doing; we cannot understand learning without observing children as they learn; we cannot evaluate our effectiveness unless we observe the impact on learning of our provision, organisation and interactions.

One way of representing these tasks is in the form of a wheel, an image that captures the cyclical nature of the practitioner's role. It is never a question, in early years care and education, of getting a job done once and for all. All practitioners are well aware of how their separate daily tasks are part of a more complex and continuous whole, an on-going cycle of improvement and renewal, leading to the development of better practice and greater expertise.

The practitioner's wheel

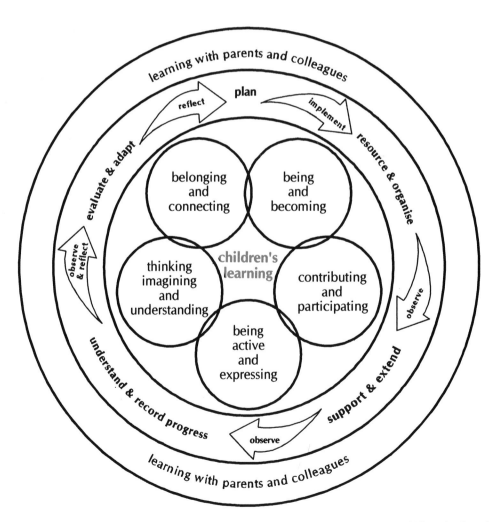

Inside the wheel, around the **foundations**, are shown the practitioners' daily tasks; the outer rim of the wheel shows an important source of information, evidence and support for these tasks. In working closely with colleagues, practitioners can verify the evidence they have amassed through observation; they can discuss the interpretations they might make of their observation; they can, together, build up an all-round understanding of each child's learning; they can use these shared understandings as the basis on which to evaluate their work. In all this, practitioners are *learning with their colleagues*.

In the same way, practitioners who work closely with parents and other carers have access to vitally important evidence of children's learning. They can compare notes and discuss the meaning of their observations, in the setting and in the home; they can think together about how best to support and extend the development of individual children, meeting their changing needs and responding to individual patterns of learning. In all this, practitioners are *learning with parents and other family members* as well as with their colleagues. Each of the key tasks represented in the wheel can be carried out more effectively within a relationship of partnership between families and practitioners.

Partnership between parents and early childhood practitioners

The concept of partnership is, however, a complex one; effective partnership is not an easy matter and cannot be taken for granted, even though the wish to work closely with parents and families is strong in early years settings. Partnership can and should take different forms, but is essentially about two equal, though often very different, parties coming together with a shared sense of purpose, mutual respect and a willingness to work together. In parent-practitioner partnerships each member will have special knowledge - the parent's specific knowledge of the child learning at home over a long period, and of the local community; and the practitioner's more general knowledge of how children develop and learn in groups. Partnership implies a two-way process with knowledge and information flowing freely both ways.

Parental involvement does not merely contribute to quality but is essential if early education is to be successful. Starting with Quality (Rumbold Report) DES 1990

Parents are the main educators of their children and should be involved in all aspects of the group, including management, in order to strengthen and build on parental responsibility and increase both enjoyment of parenting and understanding of child development. The Pre-school Learning Alliance believes parents, playleaders and volunteers are essential partners in the development of good care and education practice.
Pre-school Playgroups Association Guidelines 1993

Children's earliest learning is rooted in their immediate environment, in their family and community. Establishing a close relationship between school and community will build on and extend those experiences. Curriculum Council for Wales 1991

Partnership and the law

Not only is partnership between parents and early childhood workers good practice, it is now enshrined in legislation. The UN Convention on the Rights of the Child, (United Nations 1989) for example, requires that 'state parties shall respect the responsibilities, rights and duties of parents and where applicable of the extended family or community....to provide, in a manner consistent with the evolving capacities of the child, appropriate direction and guidance' (article 5); and also requires that 'state parties shall render appropriate assistance to parents and legal guardians in the performance of their childrearing responsibilities' (article 18).

The 1989 Children Act sees the welfare of the child as of paramount importance, and in stressing the importance of children being brought up and cared for within their own families, emphasises the importance of practitioners working in partnership with parents and children.

The 1988 Education Reform Act and the Parents' Charter also stress the need for a real partnership between parents and a child's school, and for parents to be given access to information about the curriculum being taught and their child's progress. Parents also have the right to be informed of and included in discussions about their child's progress or about any special educational needs; and have a right to meet with inspectors and make their views known to them.

Under the 1975 and 1986 Sex Discrimination Acts, the 1976 Race Relations Act and the 1995 Disability Discrimination Act parents have the right to expect equal treatment for their children in early childhood services.

Some principles of partnership

The members of the Early Childhood Education Forum who developed *Quality in Diversity* recognise the need for those who work with children to create the conditions for partnership to work as shown in the box opposite.

Working with the framework: practitioners in action

The examples that follow were contributed by members of the project; they represent a wide range of settings across the country, and a diversity of approaches to quality provision.

These examples show how the component parts of the framework, the **FOUNDATIONS** and **GOALS for early learning**, and **ENTITLEMENTS for all children**, can be used to examine the tasks of practitioners as they have been described here.

In each example, selected extracts from the foundations, and relevant goals and entitlements, are used as illustrations of the kinds of thinking and development work that practitioners can do, using the framework. They illustrate some of the ways in which the framework can be used by practitioners to enhance the quality of their work.

Principles of partnership

- respect for children as individuals, for their ability/disability, sex/gender, as members of families and as members of ethnic/racial, linguistic, social, cultural and religious groups;

- respect for the different ways that different parents have of loving and caring for their children and preparing them for adult life, according to differences in cultural practices and religious beliefs;

- willingness to relate to children and their parents in diverse ways and to share responsibility;

- respect for parents' decisions about their own lives, in particular for the choices they make about working outside the home;

- commitment to communicate on a regular basis and in as many ways as possible and in as many languages as necessary;

- commitment to listen to parents' views about early childhood settings and to take account of their concerns;

- acknowledgement that there are different views of childhood, child rearing practices and the goals of education, different views about the roles of parents and the practitioners who look after children, and that these may need to be explored and explained in open and sensitive dialogue;

- clear communication about the ways in which parents can contribute to their children's education and improve the quality of their children's experience in the setting as well as outside it;

- clear communication channels for parents and practitioners to share knowledge of all aspects of children's needs, health, welfare, individual characteristics, progress and successes in accessible language, free from jargon;

- clear procedures to support parents becoming involved in the management and/or day to day life of the setting and in contacting management and parent representatives.

Example one

Practitioners planning for children's learning

Context

Practitioners in a setting for three- and four-year-olds wanted to use the Quality in Diversity *framework in their planning.*

*They began by examining the goals and entitlements associated with **belonging and connecting**. They became more familiar with these parts of the framework by rephrasing them as questions (as shown in the lay-out below), emphasising their responsibilities in this area of children's learning. They selected the goals and entitlements that seemed most relevant to them at the time.*

They went on to use the questions they had written to help them evaluate their current practices.

Belonging and connecting

Relevant goals	Relevant entitlements
How do we help children to . . .	How do we meet our responsibility to . . .
• form mutually respectful relationships?	• work with parents in a partnership of trust?
• learn about family history?	• show respect for our families' concerns, circumstances, practices and traditions?
• learn about their membership of groups?	• act respectfully and with equal concern towards all the members of our community?

Implications for planning for children's learning

By this stage, the practitioners felt they had achieved a clearer understanding of what they were doing, and what they wanted to achieve in the future. More focussed planning could begin.

First they considered **long-term plans**. Their ideas included:

● planning for welcome: a parent and a member of staff were invited to review the setting's booklet. Was it user-friendly? Did it reflect the principle of trust? Another member of staff agreed to be in charge of making sure the entrance to the setting was friendly, and expressed the principle of respect;

- planning for partnership: a programme was drawn up of individual meetings between practitioners and parents (and other family members) so that noone was left out of the on-going dialogue that is at the heart of effective partnership;

- planning for review: the practitioners recognised that they would need to review any changes they made in their practice in order to check on their effectiveness. They worked out a realistic timescale for this process.

They went on to look at **medium-term planning**. Here their suggestions included:

- ways of including in the curriculum aspects of family histories and cultures, for example by using photographs, everyday objects from home with a treasured history, making tape recordings of songs and lullabies, inviting family members to visit the setting;

- increasing the number of local visits for small groups of children and the number of local visitors;

- allocating time to think, for themselves, about the meaning of belonging and connecting for their own relationships within the community and in the setting.

When they turned to **short-term planning**, their work became still more focused. The theme they had selected as a centre of interest for the next three weeks was babies. Several babies had been born recently to families using the provision, and there had been a great interest in doll play. They knew that one of the babies was to be christened soon and they used this as a starting point for thinking about names and naming ceremonies. They planned to:

- ask parents and other family members for information about the children's given names and how they were chosen;

- use small group discussion time with the children to talk about their names and how each name fitted in to their family's history;

- provide further resources including three new dolls who would need naming; discuss with the children how to choose their names (to signify their connection with the children and the setting); plan with the children how to celebrate their 'naming' of the dolls.

Example two

Practitioners resourcing and organising

Context
This observation was made in a setting for children from birth to school age.

Observation
Mandy (33 months) sat next to Doris (practitioner) who was talking with Omar. Omar (24 months) was playing with some books on the rug. Omar was about to begin one of his daily physiotherapy sessions to help him manage the symptoms of his epilepsy and hemiplegia. Mandy had come to join them and help - this is a regular exchange between these two children who are friends. Mandy reached for Omar's splints and began to rub his legs gently, imitating Doris's movements. Mandy then picked up the instruction book of exercises that Doris had been referring to and held it up open at the correct place so that Doris could see it more easily. Doris remarked on how helpful Mandy was being. Mandy continued to imitate and join in the physiotherapy routine with Doris and Omar. At intervals she held up the book between her legs and stroked Omar's legs gently and firmly. Doris affirmed her work and skill: 'thank you Mandy, thank you for helping'.

Being and becoming

Relevant goals	Relevant entitlements
• gaining self respect and enjoyment from their achievements	• to be supported by practitioners who are respectful of differences between children
• becoming aware of their own identities and those of others in all their differences and similarities	• to be supported by practitioners who have high expectations of all children's developing capacities
• being and becoming a communicator of increasing skill and confidence (verbal and non-verbal, gestures, sign, dialects, and languages)	• to have opportunities to take risks, to experience success and failure, and to reflect on their success and achievement
• being and becoming aware of written languages and aspects of literacy	

Implications for resourcing and organising

The most important resource for Mandy is a practitioner who knows her well and will involve her in her work. Mandy is being given the opportunities she needs to imitate and identify with the adults around her. She is gaining in self-respect and enjoyment from her achievements in 'being a physiotherapist', alongside Doris. This opportunity arose by chance in the first instance, but the staff decided that they wanted to build on it, and organise further opportunities for Mandy to take part in Omar's therapy sessions.

On a future occasion, Doris could extend Mandy's understanding by talking about other experiences Mandy has had of hospitals and treatment (her mother has recently been treated for a broken arm and collar bone). This talk may help Mandy to see connections, differences and similarities between herself and others, and in how people can sympathise with and take care of one another.

As Mandy is becoming more aware of written language (in the instruction booklet) extra materials could be provided to extend her interest. A poster, video or book, and a discussion about massage, nursing, nurturing, about people with stiff and aching limbs, would all be relevant in supporting Mandy's learning. She will, in these ways, be supported in becoming a skilful communicator, in spoken language, and in her gentle therapeutic gestures.

Example three

Practitioners supporting and extending learning

Context
This observation came from a pre-school setting with a small carefully cultivated garden area, with both flowers and vegetables.

Observation
Shona, just four, found a snail on the path just outside the building. She brought it in 'so it won't get squashed' and asked if she could look after it 'for ever'. The practitioner who worked with Shona's family group responded first by encouraging Shona, and Alex who had now joined her, to look carefully at the snail and talk about what they saw. While this was going on, another group of children who had been weeding in the garden had discovered serious snail damage to their lettuces and pansies. They rushed back into the room with the news, crying out for vengeance. Shona was distressed but calmed down when the practitioner reassured her that no harm would be done to 'her' snail. At this point, it was clear to the practitioners that the children's interests were divided; some wanted to hunt out and destroy the offending snails, and others to rescue and protect them. It seemed to be time for some thoughtful discussion and debate, of which the negotiated outcome was an agreement to find out more about the snails and their way of life before deciding what to do for the best. With support the children compiled a list of questions to which they needed answers, and the practitioners wrote at their dictation. It was agreed that the official enquiry would begin at the next session (though Shona went on admiring 'her' snail's movement inside a small glass tank until the end of the session).

Being active and expressing

Relevant goals	Relevant entitlements
• investigating the world around them	• to have opportunities for first hand experiences, physical involvement, creativity and play
• setting themselves problems and challenges	
• representing their ideas and feelings in a variety of ways	• to express a range of feelings and to be supported by practitioners responsive to those feelings
• asking questions about what puzzles and intrigues them	

The process of supporting and extending learning

- When the practitioners sat down to think about their response to the morning's events, they were almost overwhelmed by the possibilities for learning that they could see opening up in front of them. They recognised the challenge ahead: how to involve the children in focused thinking, debating, problem-solving - and in painting, dancing and making music, without, as it were, kidnapping the children's enthusiasm for their own educational purposes.

- They decided to stick very closely to the children's questions, to many of which they realised they themselves had no answers. They saw how the range of these questions would enable the children to carry out different kinds of investigations and meet a variety of challenges.

- For example, some questions about the snails' habitat and life cycle would lead the children to refer to information books, and to close observations in the nursery, in the garden and further afield. The necessary equipment (lenses, collecting jars etc.) was all to hand and the practitioners were confident in taking children outside the nursery for small group visits.

- Some of the children's questions concerned the snails' shells (Do they all go round the same way? Why do they go round?) The practitioners discussed what they would need to provide to support this area of enquiry - for example, a collection of other shells, other spiral objects, clay for modelling, the marble 'spiral' game, chalks and paint for mark-making and so on.

- Another group of questions clustered around more abstract concepts of fairness, kindness and justice. During the morning's discussion some children had reported on how snails were treated in their own gardens (*'my* Dad kills snails'), and there had been some frank exchanges about cruelty. The practitioners welcomed the opportunities for thinking about real problems, with divergent opinions being expressed. ('Are birds cruel? Cos they eat snails, and I like birds').

- Lastly, the practitioners recognised the opportunities there would be for children engaged in this enquiry to express their feelings about the different courses of action open to them. ('I'm cross with the snails, cos they ate our lettuces'. 'And I'm cross with you, because you want to kill the snails'). Before any kind of working solution could be arrived at, the practitioners realised they had the responsibility of supporting children in expressing and reflecting on some of the powerful feelings that the whole incident had triggered off.

Example four

Practitioners understanding and recording progress in learning

Context
A group of practitioners who worked with three- and four-year-olds decided to focus some observations on their children's spoken language. They were not aware of any children with particular problems but they wanted to check out this impression a bit more thoroughly. One practitioner made this observation of Jake, four years five months, with other four-year-olds in the sand pit.

Observation
Jake has a plastic bowl and wooden spoon, he is mixing the sand with the spoon. 'I'm making some nice hot soup! Oh lovely! Nice hot soup for this cold day'. He picks up a pinch of sand carefully between his fingers and sprinkles it over the bowl. 'And some cheese to melt'. Jacob comes over with a bucket of sand. 'Yep, that's right Jacob, tip it in!' says Jake. 'I'm making some nice dry powder. Ummmm!' he says stirring the dry sand with his fingers. 'You want to eat my soup later?' he asks. He mixes the sand around in the bucket with the wooden spoon. 'Anybody want some soup? Nice hot soup, do you want some? We're ready to serve. You can use your hand with this soup because it's so easy!' Shem is near by. 'Do you want some ice cream. I've got some left', he says in a deep voice, holding a plastic cone filled with sand. 'No thank you sir!' says Jake, 'but Kai does' he adds. Kai 'I want one!' 'Come on den Kai' says Shem. He gives him an ice cream cone and then goes to the other side of the sand pit. Jake turns back to his bowl. 'Nice dry sugar on!' says Jake pouring dry sand from a jug into his bowl of wet sand. He crouches and scoops up more sand in his hands. 'Right we need some nice hot spice in, Mmmmm! Nice spicy soup'. He puts sand with a spoon into two little plates on the edge of the sand pit. 'Two dinners of soup. Mmmm SOUP! are ready. One yellow one, one red one. The important thing is that we mix it really fast. It's finished now, now the first thing we have to do is decorate it'. He wiggles his finger in the top of the sand in the bowl. 'Happy birthday!' says Michael from across the sand pit. Jake turns round. 'It's my birthday isn't it?' Jake says. 'I'm going to hang some balloons up, birthday time. Whoever's birthday it is, I'll get some things ready!' says Michael cheerily. 'It's mine' says Jake moving over with his bowl of sand and putting it next to Michael, Harry and Jacob's.

Thinking, imagining and understanding

Relevant goals	Relevant entitlements
• making sense of the world through play	• to be supported by practitioners who take time to listen and to understand
• building on their first hand experiences	
• exercising their imagination	• to be supported by practitioners who follow where children lead
• communicating their thinking	

The process of understanding and recording progress in learning

- The practitioners were very surprised at the richness and detail of these children's spoken language (especially Jake). They realised that they probably had much to learn about all their children, if these few, chosen at random, could do so much more than they expected.

- They wondered if they had developed a pattern of ignoring children's play if it seemed to be progressing harmoniously, only attending to it, or intervening, if trouble seemed to be brewing. They recognised the importance of setting aside time simply to listen and to watch, in order to get closer to children's learning.

- They noticed how much Jake seemed to have learned from a cooking session he had taken part in several months ago. Soon after this session, a fault had developed on the cooker, and there had been a delay in repairing it. They decided to make sure their cooker was back in use as soon as possible, and to build regular opportunities for cooking activities into their programme. They decided they would ask the children to come up with suggestions for dishes/snacks they would like to try.

- They discussed the best way of recording what they had learned about Jake's use of spoken language and made a list of the features that seemed most noteworthy. This included Jake's skill in vividly creating a shared imaginary activity through talk, and the way in which this talk was also a way of welcoming and incorporating other children in the on-going play.

- They realised that although they had, from time to time, made opportunities to do focused observation, they had not gone far enough in making this a regular part of their practice. Nor had they thought through the ways in which they could most usefully record their observations. They decided to try out ways of collecting dated observations together, as rich and robust evidence of progress in children's learning.

Example five

Practitioners evaluating and adapting

Context
This example came from a setting for children under five-years-old. The morning session started with a range of activities set out, from which children could choose: painting, book area, sand and water play, domestic play area. At 10 o'clock the children came together for a snack, while the practitioners set up outdoor play equipment. At 10.30, the children went outside to play.

Observation
The practitioners began to notice that many children, especially the boys, did not settle well to any one activity but rather hung around, often asking if it was nearly time to go outside. As soon as the doors opened, the children rushed out, overwhelming the provision, which consisted of baskets of small equipment, balls, hoops, beanbags, skipping ropes, two small crates of construction materials, and three tricycles - the focus of the children's attention.

Competition for the tricycles was intense; there were frequent upsets, tears, fights and resentments. Parents mentioned to the practitioners that their children had been telling them 'they never got a turn', and the practitioners decided to investigate further.

They took it in turns to observe what happened at different times during the outdoor play session, and then arranged a time to meet and discuss what they had seen.

Contributing and participating

Relevant goals	Relevant entitlements
• learning to participate in the life of the group - in play, in friendship, in negotiating and resolving conflict, in celebration and in sorrow	• to become gradually more aware of what is involved in being a member of a group
• learning to understand and reflect on the impact of their choices and decisions of others	• to be supported by practitioners who welcome their contribution to shared endeavours
• learning to understand and contribute to shared rules and routines	

The process of evaluating and adapting

The practitioners' first thought on how to resolve the 'tricycle question' was to provide enough trikes for every child. Then they realised that - apart from an acute problem of space in which to ride the trikes - this would create yet more problems and would do nothing for children *contributing and participating*.

They decided to think again. They made more observations and discussed them. The breakthrough came when some of them visited another local provision and talked to practitioners there, who emphasised the way they had structured their outdoor environment to support collaborative play. This decided the visiting staff to focus on the **GOALS for early learning** given above, and the **ENTITLEMENTS for all children** that refer to sharing, membership and friendship in groups.

The changes the practitioners eventually made in their outdoor provision were a result of this different way of thinking about the issue. (Not: 'too few trikes'; but: 'not enough provision for important kinds of learning'). Working with the parents who had alerted them to the problem in the first place, they made a rota, ensuring that adults and equipment were available in the outdoor space throughout the session. The children were involved in setting up and clearing away equipment, and made innovative alterations and suggestions. The adults looked back at their observations to see which equipment had been well-used in the provision they had visited; the new equipment they decided on was chosen with an emphasis on activities that could be shared by small groups and pairs of children.

Another important development was that, in the process of evaluating and adapting, the practitioners themselves had been learning to contribute and participate. Everyone participated in the observation and analysis of the problem; everyone contributed to the course of action they decided on.

Example six

Practitioners working and learning with parents

Context
A large provision for pre-school children, serving families with a wide variety of backgrounds and experiences.

Observation
A group of parents and practitioners worked together on a project to make parents of new children in the setting feel welcome and involved from the very start of their children's attendance.

The project began when a group of parents was heard discussing a notice announcing a meeting for 'New Parents', pinned up at the entrance. Their remarks were distinctly critical, as they reminisced about their own experiences of just such a meeting. One practitioner bravely 'took the plunge' by asking the parents to tell her more. After some little time had passed and several fairly unsuccessful attempts to meet and discuss had been made, two of the parents also 'took the plunge', and spoke frankly about their less than positive experiences as 'New Parents'. Their example triggered a lot of discussion. Some of the comments logged by the practitioner were:
'We know you meant well, but we didn't know what you were on about'.
'You kept asking me what I wanted to know - I didn't know that, did I?'
*'There was a lot of talk about the parents - I wanted to know what **you** (the practitioners) do'.*
'You can never see it from the parents' point of view, you always see it from the teacher's point of view'.

*Out of this unpromising beginning developed a project in working and learning together. The parents who had taken the lead in the first frank discussion recruited five more to work in a small core team, with two practitioners, scripting and filming a video about the children's experiences in the nursery. This video would, in these parents' own words, show new parents what they **really** wanted to know, rather than what the practitioners thought they **ought** to know.*

The practitioners, still smarting a little from the frankness of the parents' criticisms of their previous practice (which had, of course, been well-intentioned and benevolent in purpose), took a minor role in the earliest stages of planning the video. In an informal discussion, however, at the end of a morning session, one practitioner showed a parent some pages from Quality in Diversity *and described how the staff group was using the framework in some inservice development work. The parent took away a copy of the pages and showed them to some of the project parents, who thought they might be useful. After further meetings, the project group decided to make a poster from a modified version of the foundations, and to use **the entitlements for all children** as the underlying structure for the video extracts they wanted to collect and edit together.*

The foundations and goals for early learning

Relevant entitlements

- to be supported by practitioners who work with parents/family members in a partnership of trust, respecting each other's concerns

- to be supported by practitioners who act respectfully and with equal concern towards all the members of the communities in which they work

- to be supported by practitioners who have high expectations of all children's developing capabilities

The process of working and learning with parents

All those involved in the project felt a tremendous sense of achievement when the video was completed, and successfully used at a 'New Parents' meeting, planned in conjunction with the project people. But there had been an emotional price to pay for this achievement. The practitioners involved realised, some for the first time, that while it is comparatively easy to trust people (in this case, parents) who tell you the good news, it is much harder - and often painful - to trust people who tell you bad news. In the process of working with parents who had critical things to say about their practice, these practitioners developed a new sense of what it means to trust and to respect other people's concerns.

They realised, too, that acting respectfully towards parents sometimes means relinquishing control, rather than assuming it. They learned that respect for the parents with whom they sought partnership sometimes demanded not *more* activity, but *less*; not a stronger lead, but a more attentive response to the parents' voices; not taking over, but letting go.

The practitioners recognised, with something of a shock, that in the course of the project, the parents' outspokenness, resourcefulness and creativity had shattered some negative stereotypes. They began to wonder if, as a staff group, they had had damagingly low expectations of parents. They asked each other how their approaches to parents in the past might have contributed to a false sense of inadequacy in some. 'How have we taught them to think about themselves?' asked one practitioner; her question stimulated further useful discussion about ways in which parents could contribute to policy making, decisions and developments, rather than just being on the receiving end of completed work.

Example seven

Practitioners working and learning with colleagues

Context

Berta, aged four years one month, has recently arrived at the setting. Her family are refugees from persecution, and have had untold difficulties in leaving their own country, gaining refugee status in the UK and finding somewhere to live. They were not English-speaking on arrival, but are quickly acquiring a working grasp of English. Berta has been in the setting for eight weeks, and still needs much adult consideration and support. There are three practitioners in the setting: Julie and Sami (both full-time) and Vibha, who works part-time. Vibha supports some of the bilingual children in the setting, but does not speak Berta's home language. However, Berta has formed a close relationship with her, and in fact the team has begun to feel that she needs help to become a little bit more independent, since she often stands waiting for Vibha to arrive, unwilling to attempt anything without her. This morning the team, having consulted Berta's parents, has decided that Vibha will occupy herself with a small group of children. If Berta wishes to join her she will have the opportunity to make relationships with other children as well. Berta is late this morning, and Vibha and her group are already involved in cooking when she arrives.

Observation by Vibha

Berta is brought in by her father, who chats briefly with Sami. He cannot stay long with Berta, but he spends a few minutes walking round the room with her, trying to get her established at an activity. He sits with her at a table and tries to interest her in a jigsaw. She sits very still, staring at the puzzle. Two other girls arrive to look at the puzzles on the other side of the table, and Berta turns her head to look at them. Her father tells her something in her own language, and she shakes her head. He pats her hand, smiles encouragingly, kisses her and says goodbye.

Berta watches the girls as they rapidly turn the puzzles out, complete them and move on to another table. She gets up and goes to look out of the glass doors at one end of the room; it is raining slightly, and as there is no sheltered outdoor play area there will be no outdoor play until the rain stops. The room is full of activity, and Berta inspects what is going on in each area. She stops by the home corner, where the same two girls are now playing doctors and nurses, wielding stethoscopes and plastic syringes as they minister to three dolls. Berta picks up a doll and holds it out to them silently. The elder girl, Katie, gives it a quick injection and says 'Thanks, Mum!' in imitation of a busy professional voice. Berta watches them for a bit, then notices me standing quite near watching her. She puts the doll back and comes and stands close to me, holding a fold of my sari. From this moment on she is my shadow again, and gets involved with the cooking activity, though without communicating with the rest of the group. But I did notice that she went on watching Katie and her friend across the room while helping with the cooking.

Berta's learning - some starting points for discussion

Relevant goals	Relevant entitlements
• forming mutually respectful relationships with close and familiar adults and children	• to be supported by practitioners who work with her parents in a trusting partnership
• learning to communicate verbally and through signs and gestures	• to be supported by practitioners who are well-informed, sensitive and responsive to her feelings and the full range of her emotional needs
• being safe from emotional harm	
• becoming a confident learner	• to be supported by practitioners who listen, watch, take time to understand, follow where she leads
• expressing ideas through imaginative play	

The process of working with colleagues

When the team of three practitioners sat down to discuss Vibha's observation notes, they were, at first, disappointed. The high expectations they had of Berta's development in their stimulating environment seemed, from this evidence, to have been unrealistic. They were all three concerned that Berta's apparent dependence on Vibha was preventing her from becoming fully involved in the carefully planned daily activities. They noted numbers of **GOALS for early learning** that seemed very remote possibilities for Berta, and questioned whether they were fully meeting their responsibilities towards her.

However, when they focused on the **ENTITLEMENTS for all children**, they began to see how much they were really doing to support Berta's learning. They realised that in barely two months they could only expect to see the beginnings of future learning, rather than massive achievements. And they agreed that the beginnings were there to see. Berta was gaining in confidence (belonging and connecting) and her willingness to communicate was increasing (being and becoming). She seemed to have taken the first steps towards becoming involved in symbolic play with the dolls (being active and expressing). Meanwhile, as Berta slowly came to terms with the enormous and difficult changes in her life, they were doing all they could to respond to her learning and emotional needs. Their combined attention, as a team, to the fine detail of every individual child's entitlements, would, in the long term, bring satisfying outcomes. The team's discussion of these issues was a difficult one; it was marked by a willingness to be self-critical rather than self-congratulatory, and by some painful feelings of inadequacy, rather than the warm glow of self-satisfaction. But by supporting each other's thinking, the team grew in a critical but confident awareness of the effectiveness of their work.

Conclusion

In this section, the framework has been used as the basis for an analysis of the part that practitioners play in children's learning. The examples show how, in partnerships with parents and other family members, practitioners can examine different aspects of their daily work, and use the foundations, goals and entitlements to monitor and enhance the quality of their provision.

Section Five
Practitioner development using the framework

Introduction

In this section we will describe how practitioners can work together using the framework, to learn more about the care and education of young children, especially about the part that adults (parents, carers and practitioners, governors and managers) play in this process. A brief discussion of some of the characteristics of effective staff development is followed by some examples that illustrate the process of using the framework in a variety of ways.

Principles for practitioner development

Lawrence Stenhouse, an educational writer and thinker who has been an inspiration to many educators working in primary and secondary schools, once described an effective classroom as a place where, every day, the teacher learns something she or he did not know before. We could translate this challenging assertion into early childhood terms: an effective setting for young children is one where, every day, the practitioners learn things they did not know before.

If we take up this challenge and argue that the learning of early childhood practitioners can and should play a central part in effective practice, it will not be enough to hope that such learning will simply come about of itself. Fortunately there is already at our disposal a good deal of experience of the ways in which adult learning can be given the encouragement and support it needs. There are all kinds of opportunities for staff groups to engage in professional development, or, as we are describing it here, to further each other's learning. For example:

- Training sessions for practitioners in one setting, organised by themselves or with the support of outside facilitators.

- Joint training for multidisciplinary groups, with practitioners from a variety of different services.

- Sessions for different groups within one community; such as parents and practitioners; governors and practitioners; inspectors, advisers, managers; and many more.

- Sessions focusing on the needs of particular groups of children; for example, children of travelling families, bilingual and multilingual children or children in hospital.

●   Training sessions to support practitioners in implementing anti-bias policy and practices.

Activities like these may need support from a consultant or adviser, or from training agencies, the local education authority, higher and further education providers and so on.

The *Quality in Diversity* framework has been produced to support practitioners taking up opportunities like these for staff development. The fundamental purpose of the framework is to ensure quality in the educational experiences of children from birth to eight. This purpose can only be realised through the thoughtful work of early childhood practitioners: their daily work, face to face with children, and their development work, when they deliberately structure opportunities for themselves to think together about their work and to learn from one another. The framework can support practitioners in both these kinds of work. The **FOUNDATIONS for early learning** can also be interpreted in terms of **adult learning**, and the ways in which adults learn most effectively together. The diagram opposite illustrates this possibility.

A framework for adult learning

Adults learn effectively when they know that they are accepted members of a group, and that their professional and personal needs (to learn, to understand, to question, to grow more certain) are respected and supported

belonging
and
connecting

Adults learn effectively when they know that their personal development is being valued, when they gain self-respect and enjoyment from their efforts and their achievements, as they grow in confidence in themselves as learners

being
and
becoming

Adults learn effectively when they know that they each have the ability and the capacity to contribute to the group's undertakings, and when there are opportunities for them to fulfil these responsibilities towards one another's learning and development

contributing
and
participating

Adults learn effectively when there are opportunities for them to take active control of their learning, directing its focus and managing its purposes. In this process, which is emotional as well as intellectual, they need opportunities to express their feelings - of doubt and hope, anxiety and enthusiasm

being
active
and
expressing

Adults learn effectively when they bring to the process their ability to think for themselves and to contribute to the thinking of others, and when they know that their growing understanding is valued and respected by the other members of the group

thinking
imagining
and
understanding

The examples that follow have been contributed by members of the *Quality in Diversity* project, and by practitioners using the trialing version of the framework. They are given here to illustrate some possibilities, not to prescribe particular approaches.

Example one: focus on a child

Practitioners learning with the framework

Context
In a provision for children from a few months old to four years, policy changes were made in the grouping of children which affected, in particular, the transition from the baby room to a family group room. Previously this transition took place as soon as the children became mobile, but as a result of the changes, the children remained in the same room until they were almost three. This meant that some of the practitioners were, for the first time, having children in their especial care who were moving from the baby stage to growing independence. As a way of monitoring the effects of this change, the practitioners in one room invited a social worker, who worked alongside them, to carry out some focused observations of selected children.

Observations
Some of these observations focused on Shayma (aged 2), who had been in the room since she was 12 weeks old. During her first year and a half of life, her keyworker had ensured that she was there to meet Shayma's every need, and had gained great satisfaction from feeling indispensable to her. The observations showed, however, that Shayma's growing independence had affected the relationship between child and keyworker. In one observation, Shayma was seen to spend sustained periods with other adults in the room. When she returned to her keyworker, Shayma found her engrossed in the care of a new baby who had just joined the group. Shayma attempted more than once to attract her keyworker's attention, but with little response. Shayma remained close to her keyworker for the rest of the session. Occasionally she stroked her arm, or tapped her leg. She did not continue her exploration of other areas of the room.

Discussion
In the discussion that followed, the staff team worked together to try to understand this observation from, as it were, the child's point of view. They tried to understand what Shayma was looking for in her new relationship with her keyworker, and what her feelings might be.

After some time, the keyworker talked about her own emotional experiences: watching Shayma's growing independence had not been easy for her. She spoke about her feelings of loss, as Shayma seemed to need her less and of the renewed pleasure she got from `being everything' to the new baby. She described how difficult she felt Shayma had become as she was developing a mind of her own, on occasions testing the boundaries that had been set for her. The easy to care for baby had become a child with a will of her own.

At this point, the practitioners turned to the **ENTITLEMENTS for all children**, and compared them with Shayma's recent experiences. They noted a number of relevant entitlements, and were able to see how the quality of Shayma's experiences was being affected.

In particular they noted the following:

> The entitlement to be supported by practitioners who . . .
>
> ● have high expectations of children's developing capabilities, giving them opportunities to take risks . . .
>
> ● are well-informed, sensitive and responsive to children's feelings and the full range of their emotional needs . . .
>
> ● listen, watch, take time to understand, follow where children lead . . .

These statements of entitlement helped them to understand more clearly how their practice was falling short of the quality they aspired to.

Next they turned to the **GOALS for early learning**, and selected some areas of concern, with the observations of Shayma in mind. As they examined the goals, they found they were asking themselves some challenging questions.

Some challenging questions about Shayma's learning

Is Shayma maintaining the close and respectful relationship she has made with her keyworker?

Is she learning to communicate her own needs, within her intimate group?

Is she learning to form new relationships with other adults in the room?

belonging
and
connecting

Is Shayma secure and safe from emotional harm?

Is she changing and developing at her own pace?

Is she becoming an independent individual with interests of her own?

being
and
becoming

Is Shayma learning to collaborate in shared activities, with familiar adults and children?

Is she learning to contribute her unique and individual thoughts and feelings?

Is she learning to understand the routines of the adults and children in the baby room?

contributing
and
participating

Is Shayma learning about the full extent of her mental and physical powers?

Is she learning to discover and investigate the world around her?

Is she setting herself challenges and learning how to meet them?

being
active
and
expressing

Is Shayma learning to make sense of her experience of the world and the adults in it?

Is she looking for explanations?

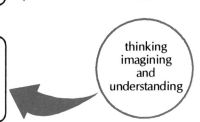
thinking
imagining
and
understanding

The discussion continues
This small group of practitioners spent many room-meetings discussing how children's needs changed over time. They realised it was not that the children needed them less, but that they needed them differently. To help them build on this new insight they used the framework.

They took the **ENTITLEMENTS for all children** and rephrased them as broad policy questions, which would be helpful in examining and evaluating their practice. They turned back to their observations of Shayma. Here the most relevant questions were these:

> How can we ensure that each child is securely supported in expressing her feelings and emotional needs?
>
> How can we ensure that **we** (the practitioners) are well-informed, sensitive and responsive to the full range of children's feelings and emotional needs?

Answering these questions brought a range of answers from different practitioners. Answers to the first question concentrated on procedures for observing children, and for making time to review the observations. The staff group also discussed the need to consult more thoroughly with parents and other family members; they realised they needed better information about children at home, and ways of making sure the information they had was sensitively used.

Answers to the second question were harder to arrive at. Some practitioners staff felt they needed to do some more thinking about children's emotional development, and the ways in which children's feelings change as they grow older. Others wanted to discuss how their own feelings about individual children could make it more difficult for them to see things from the children's point of view. They agreed to explore both these areas of concern in the coming months, and to make sure that their supervisions included opportunities to discuss these aspects of their work.

Example two: focus on a curriculum theme

Practitioners learning with the framework

Context
This example was contributed by two registered childminders who work together caring for six children (0-5 years) and six children (5-8 years). The children are from a variety of cultures and religions, including English, Danish, Indian, Iranian, German, Catholic, Muslim and Protestant. The childminders documented their work with the framework during the trialing period in the spring of 1997. The material that follows is a slightly shortened version of their written report on their work.

Observation
● *Getting started*
The overall theme for the spring half term was 'growing'. The Festivals we decided to celebrate at this time were Shrove Tuesday, Shiva Ratri, St Patrick's Day and Mother's Day. We originally decided to celebrate Holi as this is a Hindu spring festival of new beginnings and harvest. For reasons that will become clearer later, we decided that Shiva Ratri would also be appropriate and, as we did not have time to celebrate both festivals, we chose the latter. We included activities such as planting seeds, visits to a farm and a country park, creative activities such as making a farm animal display, making pretend 'binoculars' and 'magnifying glasses', enacting the story of Jack and the Beanstalk, making and eating pancakes, observing that plants are green, observing and discussing how celery sticks absorb water, and planting primulas. Everyday activities such as talking about the weather and how it helps things to grow, walking in the park and garden, looking for signs of spring and growing were also linked to our theme.

● *Linking our policies and the framework*
*Our first step was to examine our written policies, our thinking and the ethos of our child care facility against the **ENTITLEMENTS** for all children. We decided that these entitlements underpin our beliefs and our practices. We believe strongly that parents know their child best and we have a policy of sharing all information about children with their parents. Each child has a book, kept in her changing bag, in which all information about the child is written, how much a particular activity was/was not enjoyed, if the child's eating habits have changed, when the child was involved in an accident/incident, what was done to resolve it and any other significant observation made about the child. Parents are encouraged to write in this book too, conveying information from home that may be important or interesting. We have other policies such as an Equal Opportunities Policy, a Nutrition Policy, a Health and Safety Policy and others. It was decided to review our policies to ensure that they reflected the full range of **ENTITLEMENTS** for all children.*

● *Looking at our activities*
None of our activities is compulsory as we believe in allowing children to make their own decisions. We always offer children a choice of activity. For example, if the main group are painting, the Lego, the garage or the book corner are all available to children who don't want to join in, or they can simply watch the main activity, joining in when they are ready.

For each activity we do, we write up an activity sheet. These sheets include a section for the aims and objectives of the activity. Each time the activity is undertaken it is observed and these observations are written up so that we can assess whether it was worthwhile - did it reach the aims and objectives and how; have the children enjoyed the activity, and so on.

The aims and objectives of each activity were examined to see if and how they linked with the framework, the FOUNDATIONS for early learning, the GOALS for children's learning and the ENTITLEMENTS for all children. We decided to add relevant goals to this section of our activity sheet at this planning stage, so that we could include them in our evaluations of each activity.

All the activities met some of the goals. For instance, when we thought about belonging and connecting we saw how relevant these goals were to the activities that celebrated Shiva Ratri, Shrove Tuesday and Mother's Day.

Relevant goals

● learning about the groups (ethnic/racial, cultural, linguistic, religious, social) to which familiar adults and children belong.

● gradually learning about their membership of groups beyond their immediate surroundings (ethnic/racial, linguistic, cultural, social and religious).

However, we also found some gaps, and these made us think again.

Rethinking with goals and entitlements in mind

We decided to link the whole theme of 'Growing' by rewriting the story of 'Jackie and the Beanstalk'. We did this to enable us to meet the goals and entitlements in different ways; first, to challenge stereotypes, such as boys climbing, giants being horrible and scary etc. Secondly, to enable us to meet the 'linguistic' goals that appear throughout the Foundations, we decided when creating Jackie's farm display for the wall, to ask parents to write down the names of animals in their language (and teach us to say them). The languages we displayed were English, Danish and Punjabi. We sang familiar songs using Danish and Punjabi words and we translated others into German.

At this point, we discovered that we did not allow time for dancing other than simple 'folk' dances such as the 'Hokey Kokey'. To meet some of the goals in **being and becoming** we felt that the introduction of some other forms of dance would be appropriate. This was when we decided to celebrate Shiva Ratri instead of Holi. We used a cassette tape, borrowed from the library, of some Indian music. We talked to the children about the ways in which people (adults and children) move, how dancing is an expression of feelings; people dance when they are happy, although some people also dance when they are sad. We started by sitting on the mat and moving our hands, arms and upper bodies in time to the music. Then we stood up and, standing in one place, encouraged the children to use all the available space around them. We included head movements asking the children to look in different directions to make them turn their heads. One of the older boys did not want to join in, so he was offered a tambourine to shake and beat time with, which he accepted. Some of the other children then wanted musical instruments too, and they were given maracas, sleigh bells and triangles. This activity was so successful that we have decided to use it regularly. Music is coming to play a much more important place in our regular provision, not only as part of a celebration, but also giving us frequent opportunities to listen to different types and styles of music, and dancing to them.

The next development was to elaborate our own version of Jackie and the Beanstalk. Jackie lived with her mother on the outskirts of a small village. No one in the village was happy. No one sang or laughed or danced. Jackie's mother had a smallholding (this was explained for the younger children as being a small farm) with many different animals. We visited a local farm. During the week following the farm visit we made a wall display of the animals on the smallholding and named them in different languages. One day, Jackie's mother asked her to sell one of their cows because it looked too happy and contented! Jackie took the Ko (the Danish word for cow) to market. She swopped the Ko for five magic beans which her mother threw out the window. We planted kidney beans, the sunflower seeds and cress seeds and compared how quickly they grew. None of the seeds grew as quickly as Jackie's beans so the children decided they were truly magic beans. We looked at the kinds of insects that might have lived on Jackie's beanstalk and drew pictures of insects to live on our beanstalk. We made pretend 'binoculars' and 'magnifying glasses' to look at the insects in the garden. (We will use them again, when we go on our mini-beast safari in the Easter Holidays). We looked at the things that Jackie's beanstalk needed to keep it healthy, light, water, soil, warmth and how we could provide these things for our plants. We looked at why Jackie's beanstalk was so green and put one of our trays of cress seeds in the airing cupboard for three days and then compared the two trays. We talked about the things that the two trays had that were the same and the things that were different. The older children worked out that the plants needed light to make them green. We put sticks of celery into glasses of water coloured with food colouring and measured their change of colour. We gave the children drinks with straws and explained that the celery (and the roots of plants) act in the same way as their straws, sucking water up from the soil. Before Jackie could climb the beanstalk she ate a big breakfast of pancakes to keep her strength up. She found wheat growing in her mother's field, which she then ground into flour. She found eggs in her mother's hen house and got milk from the Ko (the one that she hadn't sold). Jackie made these ingredients into pancakes and ate them with jam that her mother had made from strawberries in their garden. We copied Jackie's recipe and made pancakes on Shrove Tuesday. We talked about why pancakes used to be eaten only on this day in the year and how different people eat them at different times now (such as for breakfast). After a hearty breakfast Jackie climbed the beanstalk. At the top she discovered Shiva the Hindu God of Dance (who was much bigger than Jackie which is why he was mistaken for a giant). Shiva taught Jackie (and us) to dance. When Jackie climbed back down the beanstalk she taught her mother and all the people in her village to dance and this made everyone very happy. Jackie became so happy that she planted a primula in a terracotta pot that she had painted and gave it to her mother one special Sunday to tell her how much she loved her. And they all lived happily every after.

We visited a local farm with the six younger children one morning. Unfortunately, none of the parents was able to come with us because of work commitments. We pointed out different animals using their names in the different languages that we had learnt. We sang 'Old MacDonald had a farm' (to the delight of the mini-bus driver) all the way there. This was many of the children's first encounter with real live farm animals and two of the children found it quite frightening. Lots of cuddles, not getting too close too quickly, and watching the more confident children from a safe distance soon helped and one of the two actually managed to take a turn at feeding a lamb with a bottle. The more confident children were encouraged to tell the unconfident children how the animals felt and smelt. One child offered her hand for them to smell. The children were very supportive of their unconfident friends; one child told them, 'don't worry, it not bite you'.

Conclusion
We have always put a lot of care and attention into planning our curriculum, and we have always used observation to check out the effectiveness of our provision. But we feel that the *Quality in Diversity* framework has helped us see more clearly.

- The detailed **goals** for early learning help us see **what** we want our children to learn.

- The **foundations** help us see **why** we want them to learn it.

- And the **entitlements** help us see **how** we can help our children learn.

We now use the framework in all planning of our work, with children, with staff and with parents.

Example three: focus on diversity

Context
As part of an inservice course, a group of practitioners from different backgrounds, working in a variety of settings, decided that they wanted to explore the concept, introduced in Section One of the framework, that quality and recognition of diversity go hand in hand.

They planned to work out the implications of this idea by, first, selecting an area of practice with which they were all familiar, and which could be found in many different forms of early years provision, and then looking to see if there was, indeed, quality and diversity of practice in this area. They decided to focus on just one age group, four-year-olds, and just one aspect of practice: the use of traditional fairy stories and folk tales. They started with the story of The Three Billy Goats Gruff, and observed first in their own provisions, noting how the children they worked with responded to the story, and how they extended it in various ways. They pursued their enquiry by visiting a range of other early childhood settings, such as those represented by the membership of the Quality in Diversity *project (including infant and nursery classes, some traditional, some formal, some using a High/Scope approach, a Montessori class, playgroups and private nurseries).*

On these visits they observed story-telling and children's play, and spent time with their hosts, discussing the thinking behind their practice in this area. They asked questions about the principles and priorities that informed the practice, and about the practitioners' intentions and aspirations for children's learning. They asked about different influences on each provision (of particular authors or research studies), and they compared these responses with their own understanding of the practice. They recorded their work in some detail, and brief extracts from it are given below.

Using the traditional folk tale: The Three Billy Goats Gruff - an exploration of diversity

Setting	Elements of practice	Themes in the children's learning
A	Practitioner reading from the book. Children repeating recurring phrases. Small group discussion of alternative strategies for the goats to escape. Plastic models of goats to arrange in order. Writing and drawing materials for children's own illustrated versions of the story.	Familiarity with books, handling books, conventions of print. Opportunities for word recognition. Problem solving. Use of mathematical language: position, size, order.

Setting	Elements of practice	Themes in the children's learning
B	Practitioner telling the story every day for a week (no printed version). Materials for large-scale and small-scale imaginative play - natural materials, lengths of cloth, large wooden blocks.	Appreciation of rich forms of literary language. Understanding of the grand moral themes implicit in the story. Incorporation of these themes and language in children's spontaneous imaginative play.
C	Story selected as part of group topic on *Animals*. Many other stories used from around the globe and from different cultural traditions. Welcoming book corner, globes, atlases.	Learning about the variety of the animal kingdom and characteristics of animals (ferocious lion, timid mouse, wily fox etc). Awareness of different traditions of story-telling. Early learning in world geography.
D	Story selected for its presentation of conflict and the resolution of conflict. Discussion of conflict in children's own lives. Discussion of strategies for resolving conflict. Recording by adults of children's ideas about conflict/disagreement.	Learning about abstract concepts and polar opposites - safety and danger, hope and despair, power and weakness, struggle and achievement. Learning about the place of these concepts in their daily interactions. Learning about their capacity to contribute to positive relationships.
E	Story related to topic on families. Collecting family photographs. Parents and other family members visiting to talk about their families overseas.	Making connections between familiar concepts (families, brothers, sisters) and the characters of well-known stories. Learning about differences and similarities in family groups.

Setting	Elements of practice	Themes in the children's learning
F	Puppets and model animals provided with other materials for children to recreate and reinvent the story for themselves. Large scale physical and dramatic play encouraged and supported (time and space allowed).	Children choosing the materials they need for their selected activity (after a group planning session). Using different forms of representation, with symbolic materials and physical activity (movement, dance, music). Making their own versions of familiar stories, alone and in small groups. Children reviewing their experiences, reporting in detail, comparing and contrasting.
G	Building materials for bridges and towers. String, ribbons, rope, large planks and blocks available, indoors and out.	Patterns of connecting and transporting (schemas) in children's play - in their physical activity, in their talk, in their mark-making. Children connecting points in space with movement and/or solid objects.

The purpose of this analysis was to see whether aspects of *quality* could be recognised in the *diversity* of practices represented above. Using the **FOUNDATIONS for early learning**, the practitioners tried to identify the underlying principles of the different approaches. For example, they contrasted the approach in setting A, where the emphasis was on early literacy and numeracy, with the approach in setting E.

Setting A	Setting E
Being active and expressing	**Belonging and connecting**
Relevant goals	**Relevant goals**
● practising their mental powers	● learning about family history
● working collaboratively to solve problems	● learning about their membership of family groups
● representing ideas in mathematical language	● learning about other people's membership of groups
● representing their ideas through written and spoken language	● learning to recognise the needs of familiar adults, friends and family members

These practitioners found, through their visits and records of different practices, that they understood more about their daily opportunities to create diversity for themselves. In addition, by starting with the agreed aim of looking for differences, they came to understand more about one another's approaches to quality. In their discussions, they asked each other *why* questions, as well as *what* and *how* questions. They heard, in reply, explanations connecting specific practices to specific **FOUNDATIONS** and **GOALS for early learning**. They became better able to understand how the framework could underpin quality and diversity.

Practitioners learning together: using observations

In the preceding examples, practitioners were shown using the *Quality in Diversity* framework to support their critical and evaluative work together. In some of these examples, and in others used elsewhere in this document, the starting point was an observation, or series of observations, focusing on particular children or areas of activity. Such observations need not be labour-intensive or very long and drawn out. Brief observations, carried out by practitioners in the course of their everyday routines, can be extremely revealing and worthwhile.

The essential ingredient in worthwhile observations is a focus, often in the form of a question. For practitioners using the *Quality in Diversity* framework, the focus might be one of the foundations, or a selection of relevant goals or entitlements. On the following pages are two formats for recording observations. These formats are suggestions, not blueprints; they should be adapted and modified to suit the purposes of the practitioners involved. For further discussion of observation techniques see, for example, Drummond, Rouse and Pugh (1993) and Stierer et al (1993), and the suggestions for further reading given in Appendix 3.

Quality in Diversity in Early Learning

Possible format for recording observations (1)

Date _____   Time _____   Place _____

Observer _____

Overall question: *(Foundations?   Goals?   Entitlements?)*

Focusing questions: *(about a particular child, a time of day, an activity, a group of children, an area of the room . . .)*

Names, ages etc. of children observed

DESCRIPTIVE OBSERVATION NOTES

What did the children actually do?	**What did the practitioner actually do?**

IMPLICATIONS OF THIS OBSERVATION FOR PRACTITIONERS

What questions arise as a result of this observation?

What might be done to answer them?

What was memorable about this observation?

Possible format for recording observations (2)

Selected focus	Descriptive observation notes
(for example) Contributing and participating ● participating in the life of the groups in which they live and learn; in play, in friendship, in negotiating and resolving conflict, in celebration and in sorrow. ● collaborating in shared activities, with familiar adults and with children. ● contributing their unique and individual thoughts, feelings, ideas and activities. ● learning to take their part in caring for familiar others (adults and children). ● learning to understand and reflect on the impact of their choices and decisions on others (adults and children). ● learning to understand and contribute to the shared customs and traditions that are accepted and valued in their homes and early childhood settings. ● taking growing responsibility for themselves in the groups to which they belong, as they come to understand what it is to be members of groups. (Selected entitlements could also be used as a focus for observations or series of observations)	Date Time Place Observer Children observed:

Review of evidence

Issues for discussion

Conclusion

In this section, some examples have illustrated how early years practitioners can use the *Quality in Diversity* framework to support their pursuit of excellence as they learn and work together. The examples given here, and in previous sections, do not, of course, exhaust the possibilities for practitioner development using the framework. In any case, whatever support practitioners are given, whether in material or human form, nothing can alter the fact that practitioner development is essentially in the hands of the practitioners themselves; they shape the purposes and control the focus of their learning. They modify and adapt published materials, inventing new ways of working and learning - and this framework is no exception to the general rule.

Quality in Diversity has been written by a group of experienced early years practitioners from a variety of backgrounds, all committed to its central themes and aspirations. It is their hope that the framework, however and wherever it is used, will enable practitioners to learn a new vocabulary of shared meanings, agree on the foundations of quality, establish goals for early learning and enact their responsibilities in diverse ways.

Appendix 1
Organisations in membership of the
Early Childhood Education Forum

(Most member organisations of the Early Childhood Education Forum produce their own materials on the early childhood curriculum and associated issues).

Association of Advisers for Under-Eights and Their Families
c/o Lin Marsh
33 Selwood Way
Downley
High Wycombe
Buckinghamshire HP13 5XR

Association of County Councils and
Association of Metropolitan Authorities
        see Local Government Association

British Association for Early Childhood Education
111 City View House
463 Bethnal Green Road
London E2 9QY

Campaign for State Education
158 Durham Road
London SW20 0DG

Child Care and Education Association (until April 1997)
c/o 1 Floral Place
Northampton Grove
London N1

Children in Scotland
Princes House
5 Shandwick Place
Edinburgh EH2 4RG

Children in Wales
25 Windsor Place
Cardiff CF1 3BZ

Commission for Racial Equality
Elliot House
10-12 Allington Road
London SW1E 5EH

Council for Awards in Children's Care and Education
8 Chequer Street
St Albans
Hertfordshire AL1 3XZ

Council for Disabled Children
National Children's Bureau
8 Wakley Street
London EC1V 7QE

Daycare Trust
Wesley House
4 Wild Court
London WC2B 5AU

Early Years Curriculum Group
c/o Linda Pound
55 Blackbrook Lane
Bickley
Kent BR2 8AZ

Early Years Trainers Anti-Racist Network
PO Box 28
Wallasey
Liverpool L45 9NP

High/Scope UK
Copperfield House
190/192 Maple Road
London SE20 8HT

Incorporated Association of Preparatory Schools
11 Waterloo Place
Leamington Spa
Warwickshire CV32 5LA

Local Government Association
26 Chapter Street
London SW1P 4ND

MENCAP Early Years Project
123 Golden Lane
London EC1Y 0RT

Montessori Education UK Ltd.
21 Vineyard Hill
London SW19 7JL

National Association of Educational Inspectors, Advisers and Consultants
1 Heath Square
Boltro Road
Haywards Heath
West Sussex RH16 1BL

National Association of Head Teachers
1 Heath Square
Boltro Road
Haywards Heath
West Sussex RH16 1BL

National Association of Nurseries in Colleges and Universities
Coventry University Nursery
Alma Buildings
Alma Street
Coventry

National Association of Nursery Centres
Carisbrooke Day Nursery
Carisbrooke Street
Harpurhey
Manchester M9 5EQ

National Association of Schoolmasters/Union of Women Teachers
Hillscourt Education Centre
Rose Hill
Rednall
Birmingham B45 8RS

National Campaign for Nursery Education
BCM Box 6216
London WC1N 3XX

National Childminding Association
8 Masons Hill
Bromley
Kent BR2 9EY

National Children's Bureau
8 Wakley Street
London EC1V 7QE

National Confederation of Parent/Teacher Associations
161 Lower Blandford Road
Broadstone
Dorset BH18 8NU

National Early Years Network
77 Holloway Road
London N7 8JZ

National Portage Association
127 Monks Dale
Yeovil
Somerset BA21 3JE

National Private Day Nurseries Association
Portland House
55 New Hey Road
Lindley
Huddersfield HD3 4AL

National Union of Teachers
Hamilton House
Mabledon Place
London WC1H 9BD

NIPPA - The Early Years Organisation
Enterprise House
Boucher Crescent
Boucher Road
Belfast BT12 6HU
Northern Ireland

Pre-school Learning Alliance (formerly Pre-school Playgroups Association)
69 Kings Cross Road
London WC1X 9LL

Professional Association of Nursery Nurses
2 St James' Court
Friar Gate
Derby DE1 1BT

Save the Children
17 Grove Lane
London SE5 8RD

Steiner Waldorf Schools Fellowship
Kidbrooke Park
Forest Row
Sussex RH18 5JA

Tutors of Advanced Courses for Teachers of Young Children
BCM Box 5342
London WC1N 3XX

Working for Childcare
77 Holloway Road
London N7 8JZ

World Organisation for Early Childhood Education
(Organisation Mondiale pour l'Education Préscolaire - OMEP)
144 Eltham Road
London SE9 5LW

From January 1998 representatives of the Local Authority Early Years Coordinators Network
from the following Regions were represented:
> Eastern
> East Midlands
> London
> Mersey
> North East
> North West
> South East
> South West
> West Midlands
> Yorkshire and Humber

Appendix 2

Documents from the following sources were provided by Early Childhood Education Forum members as examples of good practice.

Local authorities

Avon County Council: Education Department
Barnsley Metropolitan Borough Council: Education Department
Bedfordshire County Council: Education Department
Berkshire County Council: Education and Social Services Departments
Bolton Metropolitan Borough Council: Education and Arts Department
Bradford Metropolitan Council: Education and Social Services Departments
Buckinghamshire County Council
Camden, London Borough:Education Department
Clwyd County Council: Education Services
Coventry City Council
Croydon, London Borough: Education Authority
Derbyshire County Council: Education Department
Devon County Council: Education Department
Doncaster Metropolitan Borough Council: Directorate of Education Services
Durham County Council: Education Department
Dyfed County Council: Education Department
East Sussex County Council: Education Department
Enfield, London Borough: Education Department
Essex County Council: Education Department
Gwent County Council: Education Department
Haringey, London Borough: Education Services
Hillingdon, London Borough: Education and Social Services
Hounslow, London Borough
Humberside County Council: Education Department
Isle of Wight County Council: Early Years Unit
Kent County Council: Education Department
Kirklees Metropolitan Borough Council: Education Department
Leeds City Council: Education Department
Leicestershire County Council
Manchester City Council: Education and Social Services Departments
Mid-Glamorgan County Council: Education Department
Newcastle City Council: Education Committee
Newham, London Borough: Education, Leisure and Social Services Departments
Norfolk County Council: Education Department
Northamptonshire County Council: Social Services Department
North Tyneside Borough Council: Education Department

Northumberland County Council: Advisory and Inspection Division
Oxfordshire County Council: Education Service/National Primary Centre
Salford City Council: Education Department
Sandwell County Council: Education Department
Sheffield City Council: Education Department
Shropshire County Council: Education Services
Solihull Metropolitan Borough Council: Education Division
Stockport Metropolitan Borough Council: Education Division
Sunderland County Council: Education Authority
Surrey County Council: Education Services
Sutton, London Borough: Social Services Department
Tower Hamlets, London Borough: Teachers' Workplace Nursery Service
Trafford Metropolitan Borough Council: Education Committee
Waltham Forest, London Borough
Wandsworth, London Borough
Warwickshire County Council
West Glamorgan County Council
Westminster, London Borough
Wirral Metropolitan Borough Council: Early Years Education

Groups and organisations

Bernard van Leer Foundation
Commission for Racial Equality
Early Years Curriculum Group
Early Years Trainers Anti-Racist Network
Kids' Clubs Network
Montessori Education (UK)
National Association of Inspectors and Educational Advisers
National Childminding Association
National Early Years Network
National Private Day Nurseries Association
National Union of Teachers
Portage Association
Pre-school Learning Alliance
Save the Children
World Organisation for Early Childhood Education
 (Organisation Mondiale pour l'Education Préscolaire - OMEP)

Appendix 3
Further reading

Athey, C (1990) *Extending Thought in Young Children: A parent teacher partnership.* Paul Chapman Publishing

Ball, C (1994) *Start Right: The importance of early learning.* Royal Society of Arts

Bartholomew, L and Bruce, T (1993) *Getting to Know You. A guide to record-keeping in early childhood education and care.* Hodder & Stoughton

BBC Education in association with National Children's Bureau, Early Childhood Unit (1997) *Tuning in to Children* (Video directed and edited by S Fielden and D Selleck. Accompanying book by Tina Bruce). BBC Educational Developments

Blenkin, G and Kelly, A eds (1994) *National Curriculum and Early Learning: An evaluation.* Paul Chapman Publishing

Blenkin, G and Kelly, A eds (1996) *Early Childhood Education: A developmental curriculum.* Paul Chapman Publishing

Bredekamp, S ed. (1987) *Developmentally Appropriate Practice in Early Childhood Programs Serving Children from Birth thro Age 8.* Washington DC, USA: National Association for the Education of Young Children

Brown, M (1990-93) *The High-Scope Approach and the National Curriculum.* Set of four booklets. High/Scope UK
    1. *An introduction*
    2. *Organisation of space and resources*
    3. *Negotiating the use of time with children*
    4. *Planning the use of time with adults*

Browne, N and France, P eds (1986) *Untying the Apron Strings: Anti-sexist provision for the under-fives.* Open University Press

Bruce, T (1987) *Early Childhood Education.* Hodder & Stoughton

Bruce, T (1996) *Helping Young Children to Play.* Hodder & Stoughton

Bruce, T and Meggitt, C (1996) *Child Care and Education.* Hodder & Stoughton

Carnegie Corporation of New York (1994) *Starting Points: Meeting the needs of our youngest children. Report of the Carnegie Task Force.* New York, USA: The Corporation

Clay, J (1990) *Working with Lesbian and Gay Parents and their Children.* Washington DC, USA: National Association for the Education of Young Children

Commission for Racial Equality (1996) *From Cradle to School. A practical guide to racial equality in early childhood education and care.* CRE

Cox, T ed (1996) *The National Curriculum and the Early Years. Challenges and opportunities.* Falmer Press

David, T Curtis, A and Siraj-Blatchford, I (1992) *Effective Teaching in the Early Years: Fostering children's learning in nurseries and infant classes.* An OMEP (UK) Report. Trentham Books

Derman-Sparks, L and ABC Task Force (1989) *Anti-bias Curriculum. Tools for empowering young children.* Washington DC: USA: National Association for the Education of Young Children. (Available from the National Early Years Network)

Desforges, C ed. (1989) *Early Childhood Education.* British Journal of Educational Psychology Monograph Series, no. 4. Edinburgh: Scottish Academic Press

Dickins, M and Denziloe, J (1998) *All Together. How to create inclusive services for disabled children and their families. A practical handbook for early years workers.* National Early Years Network

Donaldson, M (1987) *Children's Minds.* Fontana

Drummond, M J (1993) *Assessing Children's Learning.* David Fulton Publishers

Drummond, M J, Eddington, M and Pugh, G eds (1989) *Working with Children: Developing a curriculum for the early years. A learning pack for people working with young children.* NES/National Children's Bureau

Early Years Curriculum Group (1989) *Early Childhood Education: The early years curriculum and the National Curriculum.* Trentham Books

Early Years Curriculum Group (1992) *First Things First: Educating young children.* Madeleine Lindley

Early Years Curriculum Group (1998) *Interpreting the National Curriculum: Developmentally appropriate practice at Key Stage one.* Open University Press (in press)

Early Years Trainers Anti-racist Network. EYTARN has a range of publications including:
    Racism: The white agenda. (1993)
    All our Children - A guide for those who care. (1993)
    Best of Both Worlds - Celebrating mixed parentage. (1995)
    Partnership with Parents: An antidiscriminatory approach. (1995)
    On the Spot: Dealing with racism. (1996)
    Travelling the Anti-racist Road (1996)

Edwards, A and Knight, P (1994) *Effective Early Years Education. Teaching young children.* Open University Press

Edwards, C, Gandini, L and Forman, G (1993) *The Hundred Languages of Children. The Reggio Emila approach to early childhood education.* Norwood NJ, USA: Ablex Publishing

Elfer, P *ed* (1995) *With Equal Concern.* National Children's Bureau

Equality Learning Centre
    ELC have reading lists on issues concerned with equality in the early years

Equal Opportunities Commission (1994) *An Equal Start: Guidelines on equal treatment for the under-eights.* EOC

Gammage, P and Meighan, J *eds* (1995) *Early Childhood Education. The way forward.* Education Now Books

Goldschmied, E (1986) *Infants at Work. Babies of 6-9 months exploring everyday objects.* (Video - 20 minutes). National Children's Bureau

Goldschmied, E (1992) *Heuristic Play with Objects. Children of 12-20 months exploring everyday objects.* (Video - 20 minutes). National Children's Bureau

Goldschmied, E (1994) *People Under Three. Young children in day care.* Routledge

Goldschmied, E and Selleck, D (1996) *Communication Between Babies in their First Year.* (Book and accompanying 25-minute video). National Children's Bureau

Golombuk, S and Fivush, R (1994) *Gender Development.* Cambridge University Press

Gura, P *ed* (1997) *Reflections on Early Education and Care Inspired by Visits to Reggio Emila.* British Association for Early Childhood Education

Hazareesingh, S, Simms, K and Anderson, P (1986) *Educating the Whole Child: A holistic approach to education in the early years.* Building Blocks Educational (Save the Children)

Henderson, A (1995) *Observation and Record Keeping in Pre-school Groups.* Pre-school Learning Alliance

Hohmann, M N, Banet, B and Weikart D P (1979) *Young Children in Action,* Ypsilanti MI, USA: High/Scope Press. (Available from High/Scope UK)

Hohmann, M N and Weikart, D P (1995) *Educating Young Children: Active learning practices for pre-school and child-care programmes,* Ypsilanti MI, USA: High/Scope Press

Holtermann, S (1995) *Investing in Young Children: A reassessment of the cost of an education and day care service.* National Children's Bureau

Hurst, V (1997) *Planning for Early Learning. Educating young children.* Paul Chapman Publishing

Hutchin, V (1996) *Tracking Significant Achievement in the Early Years.* Hodder & Stoughton

Hyder, T and Kenway, P (1995) *An Equal Future: A guide to anti-sexist practice in the early years.* National Early Years Network with Save the Children Fund

Isaacs, S (1971) *The Nursery Years.* Routledge & Kegan Paul

Jaffké, F (1996) *Work and Play in Early Childhood.* Floris

Joseph, C, Lane, J and Sharma, S 'No equality, no quality' *in* Moss, P and Pence, A. *eds* (1994) *Valuing Quality in Early Childhood Services: New approaches to defining quality.* Paul Chapman Publishing

Jowett, S and Sylva, K (1986) 'Does kind of preschool matter?' *Educational Research,* 28,1, 21-31

Lally, M (1991) *The Nursery Teacher in Action.* Paul Chapman Publishing

Lane, J 'The playgroup/nursery' *in* Cole, M *ed.* (1989) *Education for equality: Some guidelines for good practice.* Routledge

MacNaughton, G (1992) 'Equity challenges for the early childhood curriculum', *Children & Society,* 6,3, 225-240

Mason, M (1993) *Inclusion, The Way Forward: A guide to integration for young disabled children.* Voluntary Organisations Liaison Council for the Under Fives (now National Early Years Network)

Matthews, J (1994) *Helping Children to Draw and Paint in Early Childhood. Children and visual representation.* Hodder & Stoughton

Montessori Education (UK) Ltd (1995) *Montessori Curriculum for the Early Years*

Moss, P and Pence, A eds (1994) *Valuing Quality in Early Childhood Services. New approaches to defining quality.* Paul Chapman Publishing

Moss, P and Penn, H (1996) *Transforming Nursery Education.* Paul Chapman Publishing

National Association for the Education of Young Children (1991) 'Guidelines for Appropriate Curriculum Content and Assessment in Programs Serving Children Ages 3 Through 8. A position statement of the National Association for the Education of Young Children and the National Association of Early Childhood Specialists in State Departments of Education', *Young Children*, 46,3, 21-38

National Childminding Association (1993) *Training. The key to quality.* NCMA

National Childminding Association (1994) *Factfile: Childminder's handbook.* NCMA

National Commission on Education (1993) *Learning to Succeed. A radical look at education today and a strategy for the future.* Heinemann

New Zealand: Ministry of Education (1996) *Te Whāriki. Early childhood curriculum.* Wellington, NZ: Learning Media Ltd

Newell, P (1991) *The UN Convention and Children's Rights in the UK.* National Children's Bureau

Nutbrown, C (1994) *Threads of Thinking - Young children learning and the role of education.* Paul Chapman Publishing

Nutbrown, C (1996) *Respectful Educators - Capable Learners: Children's rights and early education.* Paul Chapman Publishing

Paley, V G (1979) *White Teacher.* Harvard University Press

Paley, V G (1981) *Wally's Stories. Conversations in the kindergarten.* Harvard University Press

Paley, V G (1988) *Bad Guys Don't Have Birthdays. Fantasy play at four.* Harvard University Press

Paley, V G (1992) *You Can't Say You Can't Play.* Harvard University Press

Paley, V G (1997) *The Girl with the Brown Crayon.* Harvard University Press

Pascal, C Bertram, T and Ramsden, F (1997) 'The Effective Early Learning Project. Reflections upon the action during Phase 1', *Early Years*, 17,2, 40-47

Pre-school Playgroups Association (1990) *Guidelines: Good practice for parent and toddler playgroups.* Pre-school Learning Alliance

Pre-school Playgroups Association (1993) *Guidelines: Good practice for sessional playgroups.* Pre-school Learning Alliance

Pugh, G ed. (1996) *Contemporary Issues in the Early Years: Working collaboratively for children.* Paul Chapman Publishing

Rieser, R and Mason, M (1992) *Disability Equality in the Classroon: A human rights issue.* Disability Equality in Education

Rouse, D ed (1990) *Babies and Toddlers: Carers and Educators. Quality for under threes. Papers from a seminar.* National Children's Bureau

Siraj-Blatchford, I (1994) *The Early Years: Laying the foundations for racial equality.* Trentham Books

Sylva, K and Wiltshire, J (1993) 'The Impact of Early Learning on Children's Later Development. A review prepared for the RSA enquiry 'Start Right'', *European Early Childhood Education Research Journal*, 1,1, 17-40

Trevarthen, C (1995) 'The child's need to learn a culture', *Children & Society*, 9,1, 5-19

Vygotsky, L S (1978) *Mind in Society: The development of higher level psychological processes.* Harvard University Press

Wells, G (1986) *The Meaning Makers: Children learning language and using language to learn.* Hodder & Stoughton

Whalley, M (1994) *Learning to be Strong. Setting up a neighbourhood service for under-fives and their families.* Hodder & Stoughton

Whitebread, D ed (1996) *Teaching and Learning in the Early Years.* Routledge

Whitehead, M (1990) *Language and Literacy in the Early Years. An approach for education students.* Paul Chapman Publishing

Woodhead, M (1996) *In Search of the Rainbow.* The Hague, The Netherlands: Bernard van Leer Foundation

Working Group Against Racism in Children's Resources (1993) *Guidelines and Selected Titles. 100 picture books chosen by the Working Group Against Racism in Children's Resources.* WGARCR

Working Group Against Racism in Children's Resources (1995) *Guidelines for the Evaluation and Selection of Toys and Other Resources for Children.* WGARCR

References

Curriculum and Assessment Authority for Wales/ACAC (1996) *Desirable Outcomes for Children's Learning on Entering Compulsory Education/Canlyniadau dymunol I ddysgu plant cyn oedran addysg orfodol.* Welsh Office

Curriculum Council for Wales (1991) *Under-fives in School.* CCW

Department for Education (1994) *Code of Practice on the Identification and Assessment of Special Educational Needs.* DFE

Department of Education and Science (1990) *Starting with Quality: The report of the Committee of inquiry into the quality of educational experience offered to 3- and 4-year olds.* HMSO

Department of Education and Science: Her Majesty's Inspectorate (1989) *The Education of Children Under Five.* (Aspects of Primary Education, 1). HMSO

Department of Education and Science and Welsh Office (1985) *Better Schools.* HMSO

Department of Education and Science and Welsh Office (1995) *English/Mathematics/ Science/Design and Technology/Information Technology/Music/Art/History/Geography ... in the National Curriculum* (separate booklet for each subject). HMSO

Department of Health (1991) *The Children Act 1989 Guidance and Regulations, Volume 2: Family support, day care and educational provision for young children.* HMSO

Drummond, M J Rouse, D and Pugh, G (1993) *Making assessment work. Values and principles in assessing children's learning.* NES and National Children's Bureau

Holtermann, S (1992) *Investing in Young Children: Costing an education and day care service.* National Children's Bureau

Isaacs, S (1930) *Intellectual Growth in Young Children.* Routledge & Kegan Paul

Isaacs, S (1933) *Social Development in Young Children.* Routledge & Kegan Paul

Lindon, J (1993) *Child Development from Birth to Eight: A practical focus.* National Children's Bureau

New Zealand: Ministry of Education (1993) *Te Whā riki: Draft Guidelines for Developmentally Appropriate Programmes in Early Childhood Services.* Wellington, NZ: Learning Media Ltd

Pre-school Playgroups Association (1993) *Guidelines: Good practice for full and extended daycare playgroups.* Pre-school Learning Alliance

Pugh, G *ed* (1996) *Education and Training for Work in the Early Years.* National Children's Bureau

School Curriculum and Assessment Authority (1996) *Nursery Education: Desirable outcomes for children's learning on entering compulsory education.* DfEE and SCAA

School Curriculum and Assessment Authority (1997) *Looking at Children's Learning: Desirable outcomes for children's learning on entering compulsory education.* SCAA

Statutes: *Equal Pay Act 1970*
              Sex Discrimination Acts 1975 and 1986
              Race Relations Act 1976
              Education Reform Act 1988
              Children Act 1989
              Disability Discrimination Act 1995
              Nursery Education and Grant-Maintained Schools Act 1996
              (Statutes are available from The Stationery Office)

Stierer, B and others (1993) *Profiling, Recording and Observing. A resource pack for the early years.* Routledge

United Nations (1989) *The Convention on the Rights of the Child. Adopted by the General Assembly of the United Nations on 20 November 1989.* Geneva: Defence for Children International and the United Nations Children's Fund